I0532167

THE TRANSCENDENT CHRIST

"This series of essays offers rich theological reflections prompted by the Book of Hebrews. Each essayist shows how the argument of Hebrews is illumined by St. Thomas's commentary and the light that living Tradition sheds, especially on the Sacrifice of the Mass and our celestial High Priest. I especially appreciated the introductory essay by Dr. Schmiedicke in defense of Paul's authorship."

—SCOTT HAHN, editor of *Ignatius Catholic Study Bible: The Letter to the Hebrews*

"According to St. Thomas Aquinas, the Epistle to the Hebrews—traditionally and, I hold, correctly attributed to St. Paul—is a window into the transcendence of the Lord. His transcendence manifests itself in a special way in the Mass, and it is Hebrews that lays out the sacrificial basis of this most exalted sacrament. But Hebrews does more than that, as these essays show. The contributors offer unexpected insights, with ramifications well beyond the Mass. Despite my familiarity with the Epistle, I found myself repeatedly surprised—and delighted. That will be the reaction of any reader, whether he is coming to the sacred text for the first time or the hundredth."

—KARL KEATING, Founder of *Catholic Answers*

"The book of Hebrews is often a neglected gem of the New Testament, rich with complex imagery, liturgy, and theology from the Old Covenant. It can be daunting. *The Transcendent Christ* delves into these treasures, illuminating Christ's fulfillment of every expectation—typology, sacrifice, His divinity, His eternal priesthood. Especially persuasive is the argumentation for Pauline authorship. The editors have done us a great service collecting essays that unlock the treasures of the New Covenant."

—STEPHEN K. RAY, author of *St. John's Gospel: A Bible Study and Commentary*

"What a joy to immerse oneself in such a collection—accomplished scholars employing their exegetical and theological acumen to drill down into the inspired text of Hebrews, unearth its treasures, and bring them to bear upon a far-ranging field of questions. Reading these essays is akin to eavesdropping on the great universities of the past."

—**SHANE KAPLER**, author of *The Epistle to the Hebrews and the Seven Core Beliefs of Catholics*

The Transcendent Christ

ST. PAUL'S
LETTER TO THE HEBREWS

Edited by
JOHN P. JOY
and
PETER A. KWASNIEWSKI

Os Justi
Press

Copyright © 2026 Os Justi Press
This book is a revised and expanded edition of a book
originally published in 2017 by Libri Albertini of the
Saint Albert the Great Center for Scholastic Studies.
Republished with permission.

All rights reserved.

No part of this book may be reproduced, stored in a
retrieval system, or transmitted in any form, or by any
means, electronic, mechanical, photocopying, or otherwise,
without the prior written permission of the publisher, except
by a reviewer, who may quote brief passages in a review.

Os Justi Press
P.O. Box 21814
Lincoln, NE 68542
www.osjustipress.com

Send inquiries to
info@osjustipress.com

ISBN 978-1-965303-88-7 (paperback)
ISBN 978-1-965303-87-0 (hardcover)
ISBN 978-1-965303-89-4 (ebook)

Layout by Michael Schrauzer
Cover by Julian Kwasniewski
Benedetto Carpaccio, *Adorazione del nome di Gesù
tra San Giovanni Battista e San Paolo* (detail),
Wikimedia Commons

There is none like you among the gods, O Lord,
nor are there any works like yours.

PSALM 86:8

CONTENTS

PREFACE TO
THE NEW EDITION

UNDER THE TITLE *PRÆLECTIONES ET Quæstiones Disputatæ on St. Paul's Letter to the Hebrews*, Libri Albertini published in 2017 the Proceedings of the Summer Theology Program of the Saint Albert the Great Center for Scholastic Studies that had been held from July 10 to 24, 2016 in Norcia, Italy.

Due to the quality of the content, we have decided to republish this book in a way that makes it available to a much broader audience. The entirety of the first edition is included, with minor revisions. To it has been added, as opening chapter, an essay written specifically for this occasion by Dr. Nathan Schmiedicke, Professor of Exegesis at Our Lady of Guadalupe Seminary in Denton, Nebraska, and, as an appendix, Christopher Owens's presentation of St. Thomas Aquinas's *divisio textus* of the Letter to the Hebrews, from the saint's commentary on the same.

This second and expanded edition is published with the permission of the original editor John P. Joy and of Christopher Owens, who was head of the Center.

Peter A. Kwasniewski
January 6, 2026
Epiphany of the Lord

PREFACE TO THE
ORIGINAL EDITION

SOME FIFTY PEOPLE GATHERED IN NOR-
cia, Italy in July of 2016 to take part in the fifth annual
Summer Theology Program of the Albertus Magnus Center for Scholastic Studies (AMCSS). The theme of that
year's program was "The Transcendent Christ: St. Paul's
Letter to the Hebrews." The Epistle to the Hebrews itself
was the principal object of study for two weeks, read
with the aid of St. Thomas Aquinas's commentary on
the same. The daily rhythm of the program integrated
academic study directed by the Fellows of the AMCSS
with prayerful participation in the spiritual and liturgical
life of the Benedictine Monks of Norcia. The peaceful-
ness of the picturesque town, the tremendous natural
beauty of the landscape, and the magnificence of the
Italian cuisine put the finishing touches on the experience, punctuated by pilgrimages to Assisi, Cascia, and
the eternal city of Rome.

According to St. Thomas Aquinas, the Epistle of St.
Paul to the Hebrews treats principally of the transcen-
dence of Christ as the head of the Mystical Body, the
Church:

> The matchless work of Christ is threefold: one
> extends to every creature, namely, the work of
> creation: "All things were made through Him"
> (Jn. 1:3); a second extends to the rational crea-
> ture, who is enlightened by Christ, namely, the
> work of enlightenment: "He was the true light
> which enlightens every man that comes into
> the world" (Jn. 1:9); the third extends to justi-
> fication, which pertains only to the saints, who
> are vivified and sanctified by Him, that is, by
> life-giving grace: "And the life was the light of
> men" (Jn. 1:4)... The transcendence of Christ

is thus clearly shown in our text; and this is the subject matter of this epistle to the Hebrews.[1]

Each academic day of the program included a morning seminar, an afternoon seminar, and a lecture. The lectures were designed to complement the seminar studies by delving more deeply into particular topics or issues raised by the work being studied. These lectures are collected and published in this volume together with the proceedings of the scholastic disputation with which the program culminated.

The first lecture[2] takes its starting point from the theme of sacrifice, which prevails throughout the Letter to the Hebrews. John Joy, one of the founders of the AMCSS and its current president, presents St. Thomas Aquinas's teaching on the sacrifice of Christ on the cross as an act of vicarious satisfaction and contrasts this against the typically Protestant doctrine of penal substitution.

Fr. Thomas Crean of the English Dominican Province takes up the difficult question of the precise relationship between the sacrifice of Christ on Calvary, which was offered "once for all" (Heb. 10:12), and the sacrifice of the Mass, which is offered daily throughout the world by asking the question, "How is the Mass a Sacrifice?"

The Letter to the Hebrews is rich in liturgical themes and symbolism. Byzantine priest Fr. Yosyp Veresh offers a brief summary of the layers of symbolism in the First Entrance of the Holy Synaxis in the mystagogical writings of St. Maximus the Confessor.

This is followed by a discussion of the biblical and liturgical typology in the Letter to the Hebrews by Fr. Cassian Folsom, a member, and at that time the Prior, of the Benedictine Monastery of Norcia. This takes the form of a detailed commentary on chapters 8–10 of the letter,

---

[1] St. Thomas Aquinas, "Prooemium," *Super Epistolam B. Pauli ad Hebraeos Lectura.*

[2] In the present edition, this is the second chapter.

with reference to the shadows of the Old Testament and the living icons of the Christian liturgy.

Continuing with the theme of the liturgy, Dr. Peter Kwasniewski discusses the Christian liturgy as a *sacrificium laudis*, a "sacrifice of praise" (Heb. 13:15; cf. Roman Canon). While the Mass itself is, of course, the sacrifice of praise *par excellence*, Dr. Kwasniewski also draws special attention to the praying of the Divine Office as an analogous sacrifice of praise.

Br. Evagrius Hayden O.S.B. delves deeply into the nature and necessity of faith, taking as his point of departure the famous text: "Now faith is the substance of things hoped for, the evidence of things that appear not" (Heb. 11:1). Drawing on his monastic experience of the psalter he weaves the texts of the psalms throughout his discourse on faith.

The final lecture is given by Daniel Lendman. Returning to the theme of Christ's transcendence, which Aquinas regards as the principal object of the Letter to the Hebrews, Daniel considers the various ways in which Christ can be said to be head of the Church and head of all mankind.

The proceedings of the scholastic disputation, with the masterful responses of Rev. Dr. Thomas Crean, O.P., to the three disputed questions, bring this volume to a close. They are not to be missed.

John P. Joy
March 7, 2017
Feast of St. Thomas of Aquinas

1

The Pauline Authorship of Hebrews

NATHAN SCHMIEDICKE

ST. PAUL WROTE THE LETTER TO THE HEBREWS.
Or not. Or, there is some more complicated reality at
work in the human authorship of this most remarkable
of New Testament commentaries on the Old Testament.[1]

St. Thomas Aquinas, in the introduction to his commentary on Hebrews, recognized the ancient sources of
this debate:

> Before the Council of Nicaea, some doubted that
> this was one of Paul's epistles for two reasons:
> first, because it does not follow the pattern of
> the other epistles. For there is no salutation and
> no name of the author. Secondly, it does not
> have the style of the others; indeed, it is more
> elegant. Furthermore, no other work of Scrip-
> ture proceeds in such an orderly manner in the
> sequence of words and sentences as this one.

---

[1] Letter-writing in the ancient world was often much more complex than a man with paper, quill, and ink writing a text at a
single sitting. For example, if we ask the question "Who wrote
Romans?" the straightforward answer would be "Paul." Romans
itself, however, indicates the complexity when it says that it was
rather the otherwise unknown Tertius who wrote it (Rom 16:22),
even though Paul authored it. See also 1 Peter 5:12 where Peter indicates similarly that it is "by Sylvanus" that he writes. Everything
we mean by dictation, stenography, ghostwriting, collaboration,
authorial guidance, and secretarial help, plus translation, are
potential components of historical biblical authorship. See Jerome
Murphy-O'Connor, *Paul the Letter-Writer: His World, His Options,
His Skills* (Liturgical Press, 1994).

He also gave his own and others' opinions about the question of authorship:

> Hence, they said that it was the work of Luke, the evangelist, or of Barnabas or Pope Clement. For he wrote to the Athenians according to this style. Nevertheless, the old doctors, especially Dionysius and certain others, accept the words of this epistle as being Paul's testimony . . . But Luke, who was a skillful writer, translated this ornate Hebrew into Greek.

Modern scholarship has also contributed its own candidates for author of this text. Aside from Luke, Barnabas, or Clement, we also have Aquila, Priscilla, Apollo, or Silas to consider. Or, somebody else who was a disciple of Paul who wished to, or had to, remain anonymous. Whatever the merits of these proposed candidates, the key is that they tend to have one thing in common — they were people closely associated with the mission and thought of St. Paul. Why?

This list of Paul's close associates as possible authors of Hebrews is the manifestation in the history of scholarship of the general experience of anyone who reads the text in its traditional canonical Pauline context.[2] Hebrews is like Paul.[3] It is also unlike anything else we have from Paul. As St. Thomas indicates in his introduction, Hebrews is Paul, but "more elegant."

So, what are we to think, and does it really matter? I think that it does matter, but I am also sympathetic

---

[2] By which I mean two things: first, that in the final form of the NT canon, Hebrews comes at the end of Paul's letters; second, that in the manuscript tradition, Hebrews is, tellingly, never placed anywhere other than with Paul's letters. See W. H. P. Hatch, "The Position of Hebrews in the Canon of the New Testament," *Harvard Theological Review* (1936): 133–51.

[3] Even down to using uniquely Pauline rhetoric and phraseology throughout, as shown, among others, in the recent work of David Alan Black, *The Authorship of Hebrews: The Case for Paul* (Energion, 2013), 3–23.

to those who might be bewildered or annoyed by the
question and its myriad potential answers. My experience
has been that most people, after learning about the issue
and its complexity, tend to take a version of Origen's
purported view of the matter as the safest, even if not
the most enlightening. Eusebius records Origen as having
written about Hebrews: "But who wrote the epistle, in
truth God knows," and this is taken to mean that Origen
was agnostic about Paul's authorship.[4]

Although I do not propose to show what only God
knows—the detailed mechanics of how Hebrews was
authored and written down—I do propose to revisit
the question of Paul's authorship of Hebrews with one
addition that I have not yet found explicitly and in detail
in the scholarly discourse on the subject. This addition,
intended to throw light both on the authorship question
and on the letter as a whole, is this: to look more closely
at what the text of Hebrews itself indicates about its first
intended readers, and then to look at what this adds to
the picture of a complex Pauline authorship such as that
envisioned by St. Thomas. In other words—What does
what is written and *how* it was written tell us regarding *for*

---

[4] Eusebius, *Hist. Eccl.* 6.25.11–14. Origen accepted Paul's authorship
of Hebrews, but this text has sometimes been cited as an example of early doubt regarding Paul's authorship of Hebrews, as if
Origen were saying, "God alone knows who authored this letter."
What Origen is expressing, however, is essentially the same as St.
Thomas's opinion. He questions only whether Paul is the one
who physically wrote the epistle as we have it. The thought and
authorship, according to Origen, is definitely Paul, as the context
of the quotation makes clear: "But as for myself, if I were to state
my own opinion, I should say that the thoughts are the apostle's,
but that the style and composition belong to one who called to
mind the apostle's teachings and, as it were, made short notes of
what his master said. If any church, therefore, holds this epistle as
Paul's, let it be commended for this also. For not without reason
have the men of old time handed it down as Paul's." Black (*The
Authorship of Hebrews*, 33–38) also provides an appendix of seventeen
separate citations from five different writings of Origen in which
he refers to Hebrews as Paul's.

whom it was written and ultimately *who wrote it*? Is Hebrews "Paul-yet-different" not because someone else authored it, but because its *sitz im leben* is substantially different than every other letter Paul wrote? Form follows function, and if the form of this letter is "more elegant" I would hazard that the reason for this is that its function is of a higher order—specifically, as we will see, the high-priestly order of Melchizedek operative in the new covenant of Jesus Christ, but for a very specific group of people.

Hebrews indicates in many and various ways—subject matter, tone, style, allusions, and explicit address—that the reason it is "Paul-yet-different" is that Paul wrote it to a special class of people in a special situation. They were Hebrews who had been priests of the Old Covenant, the Levitical and Aaronic order, but whose Levitical-Aaronic priesthood had been fulfilled and elevated by entering the new covenant priestly order of Melchizedek under the High Priesthood of the new covenant in Jesus Christ. These Levitical-now-Melchizedekian priests of the new covenant in Jesus the Christ were still living in Jerusalem, or very near it, close in time to 65 AD, the year that saw the beginning of the war that destroyed the Second Temple in 70 AD. That destruction, occurring forty years after the initiation of Christ's public ministry, was to be the enduring, divinely prophesied sign that the order of the old covenant had ended in the fulfillment of the new covenant. Hebrews would be unnecessary had the destruction already occurred.

Their immediate historical situation seems to have been that they were being pressured by former colleagues of the old covenant who had not accepted Christ as the Jewish messiah, or by colleagues who had accepted Christ, but who did not realize the full ramifications of the new covenant for the practice of their new covenant priesthood. The upshot of the pressure was to get them to return to their former mode of priestly ministry and sacrifice in the temple, within the order of the old covenant.

If we allow a brief anachronism, we can say this more briefly. These old-now-new-covenant priests had formerly offered temple sacrifice, but since their conversion and ordination into Christ's priesthood, they had been offering the sacrifice of the new covenant, the Mass. Now they were being pressured to stop and to revert. Paul wrote Hebrews to tell them not to revert and to keep offering the Mass.

Two main aspects of the letter indicate this. The first is *how* Paul talks to them (Part I). The second is *what* Paul talks about with them (Part II).

PART I. HOW PAUL TALKS TO NEW COVENANT HEBREW PRIESTS

The main reason St. Luke comes up first in Origen and Thomas as a candidate for involvement in the writing of Hebrews is not only that Luke was Paul's companion, but also that he was Paul's main champion. Luke's Gospel and Acts of the Apostles constitute a two-volume apologia for the work of God in and through the most surprising character in early Christianity — St. Paul. They are a canonized commentary on the life and thought of this Hebrew Apostle to the gentiles.

Having prepared the way by recording Jesus' prophecy regarding the temple's destruction and its connection to the coming "times of the gentiles" (Luke 21:24), Luke reveals in Acts 6 something about the priests of the Old Covenant that no one else does. After Pentecost, the Apostles were still present in Jerusalem and still preaching Jesus as the Christ daily, *in the temple* (Acts 5:42). Shortly after this and his record of the ordination of the first deacons in the church, Luke also mentions that "the word of God increased; and the number of the disciples multiplied greatly in Jerusalem, and *a great many of the priests* were obedient to the faith" (Acts 6:7).

Who were these priests who heard the apostles preaching Christ in the temple and who thereby became "obedient to the faith"? What became of them? The answer, if we take Luke's larger purpose and the evidence of Hebrews into account, is that they were priests who did not stop being priests when they became "obedient to the faith." Rather, their old covenant priesthood had been fulfilled in new covenant priesthood, and among these priests were those to whom the Apostle to the gentiles, writing from Italy[5] (Heb 13:24), was addressing his letter to the Hebrews.

We know from Romans 9-11 how important the conversion of "all Israel" (Rom 11:26) was to the Apostle to the gentiles, and that he saw his mission to convert the gentiles, not as an end in itself, but as inherently bound up with his painfully ardent desire for the conversion of all Israel (Rom 9:3; 11:13-14) and the completion of the whole work of Christ for the world (Rom 11:15). The conversion of Israelite Levitical priests to Christ and His new covenant priesthood must have had a special significance and importance for the Apostle to the gentiles.

One way of beginning to see these priests not merely as having entered the new covenant, but also as a special priestly class within the Christian new covenant movement, is that Paul uses specific forms of address and inclusion to set them apart from the general body of Christians when he says, "Therefore, holy brethren (*adelphoi hagioi*), who share a heavenly call, consider Jesus, the apostle and high priest of our confession (*homologia*)" (Heb 3:1).

There are two points here. The first is that Paul addresses them not with his usual "brethren" but rather with "holy brethren" (*adelphoi hagioi*), an otherwise unknown designation in the New Testament, indicating a class within the church set apart from the laity.[6] The

---

[5] Given Luke's evidence (Acts ends with Paul in Rome), as well as Paul's own stated intentions in his letter to the Romans (Rom 1:8-15), he is probably writing not only from Italy, but, within Italy, from Rome.

[6] Some manuscripts of 1 Thess 5:27 also use this form of address, though, if authentic, it could simply be another example of the same priestly-address phenomenon. An echo of the same phrase

specific language of holy, as in "*Holy* to the Lord" was the designation of the high priest (Exod 28:36) and of priests generally (Lev 21:6) in the Old Covenant. And although "holy" was also a designation of the whole people (Exod 19:6), the reality of being set apart within all Israel as representative firstborn-sons-of-Israel was a divinely ordained characteristic specific to Levite males (Num 3:12).[7] Moreover, though most translations render the plural *hagiois* in Heb 6:10 as "saints" or "holy ones" as referring to people, it is just as likely a reference to the holy things/places that these men are "serving" as it is frequently used throughout the letter in referring to the "holies" of the Old Covenant.[8] "For God is not so unjust as to overlook your work and the love which you showed unto His Name in serving *the holy things*, as you still serve" (Heb 6:10). It could also, of course, be an intentional double-entendre incorporating both an old and new covenant perspective: Levites/priests are the holy ones who have care of the holy things for the holy people.

The second point is that, having established the priestly class by this special form of address, Paul intensifies his designation by telling these holy brethren who "share in a heavenly call" to consider Jesus "the high priest of *our homologia*." I would suggest that this is again a statement of a special reality within the general confession of Christianity. The "heavenly calling" and "our

---

may be present also in Col 1:2 (*tois in Kolossais agiois kai pistois adelphois in Christo*), "to the holy and faithful brethren in Christ," though this could also be seen as indicating distinctions: "to the holy ones [priests?] and to the faithful brethren [laity?]."

[7] Likewise, the claim of general holiness for all the people, though true in terms of the general vocation, never bodes well (Exod 19:6; Num 16:3), and ends with a miraculous reinstatement of the distinction between Levite/priest and people. See Exod 32:28–29; Numbers 17; cf. Heb 9:4, which likewise draws attention to Aaron's rod that budded as a sign of his distinction from the people as priest.

[8] For example, Heb 8:2; 9:1–3, 8, 12, 24, 25; 10:19. Heb 13:24 is an exception, where it is part of a greeting.

confession" is specifically that of a common professed sharing in a call to be ministerial priests, in the service of the high priesthood in the new covenant of Jesus Christ. As a word, *homologia* is relatively rare in the New Testament, appearing three times in Hebrews (Heb 4:14; 10:23), and elsewhere only twice, both times, however, in Paul (2 Cor 9:13; 1 Tim 6:12–13), and both times having intimate connections with the liturgy[9] and the priesthood.[10] Its six appearances in the LXX all have to do, not with general verbal or interior confession or profession of a doctrine or belief, but with a vow, specifically

---

[9] In 2 Corinthians 9, Paul is telling the Corinthians that they need to take up a collection, essentially to do for "the holy ones" in Jerusalem what all the Israelite tribes of old were supposed to do—provide for the sustenance of the holy ones/Levites/priests who served at the tabernacle/temple and who offer the sacrifices for them. Once translated literally, this text lights up with references to what we call the Mass: "For the service (*diakonia*) of this liturgy (*leitourgias*) is not only completely filling up the needs of the holy-ones (*hagion*), but also is overflowing through many eucharists (*eucharistion* [plural!]) to God."

[10] In 1 Tim 6:12–13 the good confession given by Timothy cannot be simply that he believes Jesus is Lord. Since Paul, in a rare reference to the public ministry of Jesus, correlates Timothy's *homologia* precisely with that of "Christ Jesus who in his testimony before Pontius Pilate made the good *homologian*," it must be something more. The usual answer is that just as Jesus witnessed to the truth of his kingship before Pilate, so Timothy likewise confessed the kingship of Christ. This is true as far as it goes, but it does not go far enough because it is precisely in being condemned to death by Pilate and by consummating his self-sacrifice on the Cross that Jesus testifies to the truth of his kingdom. It is not merely a verbal confession of a spiritual kingdom, but a physical act of sacrifice that establishes and consummates that kingdom and that testifies to the truth (John 18:7; 19:30). The good confession of Jesus before Pilate was a reference to his vow to offer the sacrifice of Himself. Paul goes on to exhort Timothy to "keep the commandment [singular!] ... until the appearing of our Lord Jesus Christ." What singular commandment is there connected with the coming of the Lord? For Paul it cannot be anything but eucharistic: "Do this in remembrance of me ... for as often as you eat this bread and drink this cup, you proclaim the death of the Lord until he comes" (1 Cor 11:23–26).

a vow to offer sacrifice (Lev 22:18; Deut 12:17; Jer 44:25 [twice]; Ezek 46:12; Amos 4:5). Hence "our confession" in Hebrews can be understood similarly as Paul speaking to fellow priests of the new covenant about their common priestly vow and obligation to offer the sacrifice of the new covenant on behalf of the people entrusted to them.

Paul remarkably includes himself in this priestly *homologia* and sees the seriousness with which he is obligated by sacred vow to offer sacrifice (cf. 1 Cor 11:23–36). His obligation to sacrifice as a priest flows from the same obligation set upon Christ Himself:

> For every high priest chosen from among men is appointed to act on behalf of men in relation to God, to offer gifts and sacrifices for sins ... he is obligated both for himself and for the people to offer sacrifice ... so also Christ did not exalt himself to be made a high priest, but was appointed by him who said to Him "Thou art my Son..." (Heb 5:1–5).

Moreover, shortly after this in Hebrews, Paul points out that the divine declaration "Thou art my Son" was confirmed on oath by God who swore, "Thou art a priest forever according to the order of Melchizedek" (Ps 110:4; Heb 5:10). Hence, the vow to offer sacrifice for the people, to which these men have been called and to which they have bound themselves, flows from that vow by which Christ also was bound as firstborn son and high priest, by the formal oath-swearing of the Father recorded in Psalm 110. Levites and priests of the old covenant were also representative servant firstborn sons (Num 3:12). This solemn reality is what Paul is recalling these priests to with his references to their ministerial new covenant priestly *homologia*.

This becomes clearer later in the letter where Paul refers to *homologia* again in 4:14 and 10:23, both times reminding these priests of their vowed obligation to offer sacrifice, participating thereby in the once-for-all sacrifice of Jesus the high priest. Both passages are predicated in terms of the high-priestly privilege and duty of entering the holy of holies:

> Since, then, we have a great high priest who has passed through the heavens, Jesus the Son of God, *let us hold fast* our *homologias* (Heb 4:14).

> Therefore brethren, since we have confidence to enter the holiest in the blood of Jesus, by the new and living way which he opened for us through the curtain, that is, through his flesh, and since we have a great priest over the household of God, *let us draw near* with a true heart in full assurance of faith, with our hearts sprinkled clean from an evil conscience and our bodies washed with pure water.[11] We must hold fast the *homologian*... (Heb 10:19–23).

The second passage above, which I take to be the lead-up to the climax of the letter in chapter 10, predicates this entry into the holy of holies in terms explicitly eucharistic—the flesh and blood of Jesus.[12] That this is referring not simply to a creative exegesis of the Yom Kippur liturgy in light of Jesus' ascension into heaven (though it is that too), but specifically to the repeated[13] physical

---

[11] This can be taken in general as a baptismal reference, but it is also specifically Levitical and has to do with the ablutions that were part of priestly ordination in the old covenant (Lev 8:6).

[12] Notably it is through (*dia*) the flesh but in (*en*) the blood that the priest enters the holy of holies, as if indicating that "the holiest" is not achieved until the completion of the double consecration of flesh first, and through this, in the blood. Earlier in the letter, Paul likewise had paired "flesh and blood" as the nature of humanity, and therefore the reason both for the incarnation and for the eucharist in two species as indicating both the full humanity, but also the real death, of the Lord, and through His death, victory over the devil: "Since therefore the children share in flesh and blood, he himself likewise partook of the same nature that through death he might destroy him who has the power of death, that is, the devil..." (Heb 2:14).

[13] Repeated, as indicated in the New Testament, at least weekly on the Lord's Day (1 Cor 16:2; Rev 1:10), and perhaps even daily,

event of the church's eucharistic gathering, becomes clear in the punchline to this passage which is also the essential moral imperative of the whole letter: "Let us [i.e., priests] consider how to stir up one another to love and good works." If we ask "Which good works?" Paul answers in the following sentence: "Not neglecting to meet together, as is the habit of some, but encouraging one another, and all the more as you see the Day drawing near" (Heb 10:23–25). In other words, encourage one another not to neglect to offer the Mass.

This exhortation to fulfill their common *homologia* and to keep offering what we call the Mass is the main point of the latter portion of the letter. When Paul says in Heb 12:15 that his addressees must be "overseeing (*episkopountes*) that no one fail to obtain the grace of God" we should ask: Who oversees people obtaining the grace of God except those who have the power to dispense that grace? And, who would need to be told to do so except those who were being pressured not to do so? That this has specifically eucharistic implications is seen not only in his

---

as indicated by Luke (Acts 2:42–46). Hebrews also indicates the "continual" nature of the new covenant offering. Though often translated differently in Heb 7:3; 10:1, 10:12, 10:14 the phrase *eis to dienekes* [lit. "unto the carrying through"] with a basic meaning of "continually" refers both to the yearly continual sacrifices of Yom Kippur in 10:1 and also to Christ's sacrifice which is *continually* perfecting those who are being sanctified (Heb 10:14). Moreover, when Paul says in Heb 10:11–14 of the old covenant that "every priest stands daily at his liturgizing, offering *continually* the same sacrifices which can never take away sins," the contrast he goes on to draw with Christ is that Christ offered one sacrifice that is continually perfecting—continually being applied—to those who are being sanctified. St. Thomas's incisive comment on this verse in his commentary on Hebrews in instructive (emphasis mine): "But the fact that we offer the sacrifice [the Mass] every day seems to contradict the statement that it is not repeated. I answer that *we do not offer something different from what Christ offered for us*, namely, his blood; hence, it is not a distinct oblation, but a commemoration of that sacrifice which Christ offered: *do this in commemoration of me* (Luke 22:19)."

probably euphemistic mode of referring to the *eu+charist* [good + grace] as "the *charitos*" but also by his immediate marshalling of the story of Esau who "sold his birthright for one meal." This indicates the sacred eucharistic meal which is their new birthright as Christians, and their duty to confer that grace upon the lay Christian faithful. It also indicates the allure of returning to the meal (the temple sacrifices) which would constitute a betrayal (cf. Heb 6:4–6) of their Israelite birthright as new covenant priests who confer "the *charis*" that the temple sacrifices always pointed to, now that the messiah has come.

This same sacrificial food language and imagery appear again in the final chapter of Hebrews where Paul says, "Do not be led astray by diverse and strange teachings; for it is well that the heart be strengthened by grace (*chariti*), not in foods which have not benefited their adherents" (Heb 13:9). The "strange teachings" are teachings — especially Old Testament teachings — interpreted in such a way as to be estranged from what God has given in the New Testament — the reality of Jesus. They are that temple sacrificial food can benefit the eater apart from God's purposes fulfilled in Jesus the Messiah. These sacrifices, though established by God, are, if taken as final and salvific, estranged from the truth that Jesus is the Messiah, and that he has come and offered the one new covenant sacrifice that fulfills all others, when he offered Himself (Heb 7:27).

Importantly, however, the dichotomy here is not between physical temple-sacrifice food and a merely spiritual "grace" which Christians get to enjoy. Far from it. Rather, the dichotomy is between temple-sacrificial food which foreshadows and prepares, but does not fulfill, and an ecclesial-sacramental-sacrificial food referred to mystically, or euphemistically, as "the grace"[14] which

---

[14] Notably, "the grace [*he charis*] be with all of you" with the definite article, and without further qualification, is the last sentence of Hebrews. Ephesians, Colossians, 1–2 Timothy, and Titus close similarly.

does. Paul makes his eucharistic allusion as explicit as he can when he writes in the next sentence, "We [priests of the NT] have an altar from which those who serve the tent [priests of the OT] have no power [or authority = *exousian*] to eat" (Heb 13:9).

Christianity has a real priesthood, and a real sacrificial altar, and real sacrificial eating and real communion with God that comes only from *that* altar and *that* sacrifice. To neglect the priestly obligation to offer that sacrifice at that altar, and to choose instead the offerings of "the tent" would be to revert to "a shadow of the things to come" (Heb 10:1). To choose the shadow when the reality has come would be to "neglect so great a salvation" and to self-inflict the "just retribution" (Heb 2:3). Looming large on the horizon of the whole letter is the near and defini- tive end to the second temple and its sacrifices (70 AD).[15]

PART II. WHAT PAUL TALKS ABOUT WITH NEW COVENANT HEBREW PRIESTS

We have seen above the special forms of address and inclusion that support the idea of priestly addressees. The real elephant in the letter that indicates its priestly addressees, however, is simply the subject matter. The

---

[15] When Heb 3:9 quotes Psalm 95 and the forty years, it is both a reference back to the wilderness wandering of the book of Num- bers, and the death of the first generation out of Egypt, but now also a reference to the forty-year period 30–70 AD, from the inauguration of the Messiah's public ministry to the destruction of the temple should that ministry remain rejected. If Paul is writing this in the period close to 65 AD, it might not have taken a special gift of prophecy to see where the events of the Great Jewish Revolt were going to end, though these events were also prophesied, as recorded in the synoptic tradition (Matthew 24, Mark 13; Luke 21). Heb 6:8 and Heb 12:26–27 seem to be drawing on this tradition and applying it to the current situation. The temple and its sacrifices are going to end soon. Even "the Day" of Hebrews 10:25 could indicate the coming day of the temple's death, which is linked in the synoptic apocalypses both with the death of Christ, and with the death of the whole world at the end of time and the coming of the day of eternity.

subject matter and how Paul treats of it with respect to
his addressees is best explained, perhaps only explained,
by a special class of priestly addressees. Why would everything priestly, sacrificial, and liturgical of both the old
and new covenants be the focus of almost the entire letter
unless those topics were of especial importance to the first
intended readers? And for whom would this make rhe-
torical sense except priests of the old-and-new covenants?

With this in view, there is a decisive turning point
at the end of chapter 5 of Hebrews. Paul has this to say
about the first five chapters of Hebrews:

> About this we have much to say which is hard to
> explain, since you have become dull of hearing.
> For though by this time you ought to be teach-
> ers, you need someone to teach you again the
> first principles of God's word. You need milk
> not meat;[16] for everyone who lives on milk
> is unskilled in the word of righteousness, for
> he is a child. But solid food is for the mature
> [*teleion*], for those who have their faculties
> trained by practice to distinguish good from
> evil" (Heb 5:11–14).

No one would refer to the content of the first five
chapters of Hebrews, with all the intricate and elevated
biblical and liturgical exegesis therein, as baby food, or
as a mere "first word about Christ" (*arches tou Christou
logon*) (Heb 6:1). Unless, of course, Paul's addressees were
a special class of people who ought to know better and
for whom these first five chapters would be considered
the basics of priestly knowledge. For priests of the new
covenant who had been priests of the old covenant, this
ought to be basic. Paul even states that they ought not
only to understand these things, but to be able to teach
them by now, probably referencing the teaching office
that was specific to Levites and priests among the Israelites
in the times of the great reforms of Hezekiah and Josiah

---

[16] Compare the similar analogy in 1 Cor 3:2.

(2 Chron 17:8–9; 35:3), a teaching office that included specifics about what to eat or not eat (Leviticus 11).[17]

For here we have, again, the insistence on the right kind of food. The milk vs. meat / baby-food vs. man-food analogy has not only doctrinal, but also eucharistic and sacerdotal-sacrificial overtones. The language of "maturity" [*teleion*] here echoes language from earlier in the letter (Heb 2:10; 5:9) in which Paul speaks of Jesus as being made perfect [*teleiosai*], a term used in the LXX to indicate the specific kind of perfection that consists in consecration as a priest (LXX Exod 29:35; Lev 8:33).[18] Thus, it is not merely a doctrine that the "holy brethren" of this letter are being pressured to accept—that Christ is not the messiah and high priest of the new covenant (a *lex credendi*), but also a liturgical practice (a *lex orandi*)—to stop making available the eucharistic sacrifice because it is not necessary, perfect, or salvific, and to return to the old covenant sacrifices, because they are.

Thus, the rest of the letter after this point responds to these two priestly pressures with a twofold interrelated priestly focus. The two related foci of the rest of the letter are the *lex credendi*—that Jesus Christ, of the tribe of Judah (Heb 7:14), is the high priest of the new covenant according to the order of Melchizedek (chapters 6–8), and the *lex orandi*—that the sacrifice of Christ, his death, resurrection, and especially his ascension, fulfills the only universal sin offering of the Old Covenant, Yom

---

[17] Against the prevalent theory of the previous century that Christian liturgy arose out of the Greco-pagan mystery cults, Nicola Bux proposes the more probable thesis of its thoroughly Jewish roots. He suggests also that the priests of the temple, who had converted en masse to Christianity, were not only knowledgeable regarding the early Christian liturgy, but actively involved in its formation, "adattare ai contenuti cristiani il culto giudaico" [adapting Christian content to Jewish ritual]. See chapter 4 of his book *Tra cielo e terra: La mistica della liturgia orientale* (Edizioni Cantagalli, 2017).

[18] The Greek here is echoing the Hebrew idiom for priestly ordination, literally "to fill [his hands]." Cf. Exod 32:29; Lev 21:10.

Kippur (chapters 9–10), outside of which there is no forgiveness of sins.

The linchpin between these two sections of the letter is, significantly, the single longest quotation from the Old Testament in the New Testament, fittingly from Jeremiah's Old Testament prophecy of the New Testament:

> For if that first [covenant] had been faultless, there would have been no place for a second. For he finds fault with them when he says: "The days will come says the Lord, when I will establish a new covenant with the house of Israel and with the house of Judah; not like the covenant that I made with their fathers on the day when I took them by the hand to lead them out of the land of Egypt; for they did not continue in my covenant and so I paid no heed to them, says the Lord. This is the covenant that I will make with the house of Israel after those days, says the Lord: I will put my laws into their minds and write them on their hearts, and I will be their God, and they shall be my people. And they shall not teach every one his fellow or every one his brother, saying, "Know the Lord." For all shall know me, from the least of them to the greatest. For I will be merciful toward their iniquities, and I will remember their sins no more." In speaking of a new covenant, he treats the first as obsolete. And what is becoming obsolete and growing old is ready to vanish away (Heb 8:7–13, cf. Jer 31:31–34).

When Paul continues his thought beyond this quotation that links the two great foci of the letter, he says, "Now even the first [covenant] had regulations for worship and a cosmic sanctuary (*hagion kosmikon*)" (Heb 9:1). In context, this can only be read in the main mode of argumentation he uses throughout the letter, namely, the midrashic *qal we chomer* or what we call *a fortiori*. If x is true of the shadow and preparation for the new covenant in Christ, *even more so* is it true now that the new covenant has come. Thus, since the first covenant had rules about worship and a cosmic/worldly sanctuary with servant-priests under the hierarchy of the high priest, all the more so is this true of the new covenant. The new covenant is not *less* visible, priestly, hierarchical, sacrificial, place-specific, and regulated than the old covenant, but *more*.

These priests to whom Paul writes are the ones, among the Hebrews anyway, who are supposed to be making all of that clear (*lex credendi*) and making all of that happen (*lex orandi*) for the people committed by God to their care. The one force that binds the two foci of the Melchize-dekian high priesthood of Christ and His fulfillment of Yom Kippur is the reality that happens when these priests persevere in "meeting together" (*episynagogein*) [Heb 10:25] through the flesh and in the blood of Jesus (Heb 10:19–20), at the altar of sacrifice (Heb 13:10–11) that exists "outside the camp" (Heb 10:13), that is, outside of the old covenant and its temple-synagogue structure, though obviously growing up from within it.

The holy things these priests have to share with others, are, specifically "sacrifices pleasing to God" (*thusias euarestetai*[19] *ho Theos*) and the "sacrifice of praise (*thusian aineseos*)" which is "the fruit of lips confessing (*homologounton*) his Name" (Heb 13:15–16). In other words, priests who confess to be priests of Christ and the new covenant, have, as the fruit of their lips, not only words about Christ, but the very words of Christ that make Christ present. These are the words of consecration making present again and applicable to Christians of each time and all time, the one eternal sacrifice of Christ himself for all, which is nothing less than, or other than, all that we mean by the offering of the eucharist, the Mass.

---

[19] One cannot help wondering if the phrase *thusias eu-arestetai* "sacrifices well-pleasing" indicates an allusive pun on "sacrifices eu-charistic." Paul is not above punning eu-charistically in his letter to Philemon when he says in verse 11 that Onesimus was formerly "not-useful" (*a-chreston*), but is now "good-use" (*eu-chreston*), which also puns on the name of Christ, as well as on the meaning of the name Onesimus (see verse 20), which is *useful* or *beneficial*.

CONCLUSION

None of this proves Paul's authorship of Hebrews abso-
lutely, whatever "absolutely" might mean in this case.[20]
What it does do is help explain both why many recognize
Hebrews as like Paul and also unlike Paul. It also explains

---

[20] All the warnings regarding skepticism about authorship and
coming-to-be of ancient texts given in C. S. Lewis's 1959 address
to seminarians ("Fern-seeds and Elephants") are apropos here,
but especially that indicated in his account of his own and J. R. R.
Tolkien's personal experience: no one conjecturing about the coming-to-be of their works, even though close in time and culture, had
ever gotten it right. Hence, if truth is what one is after and not just
polemics, caution would counsel being skeptical of skepticism too.
    In his article "A Bluffer's Guide to Pauline Pseudonymy" (*Fr.
Hunwicke's Mutual Enrichment*, February 28, 2016), Fr. John Hunwicke notes a phenomenon which has been well-known for a long
time, yet which is inexplicably (or perhaps not so inexplicably)
ignored by many biblical scholars—namely, that the same stylistic
analysis which "proves" that St. Paul did not write many of the
letters attributed to him also "proves" any number of manifestly
absurd things about other bodies of literature. It has been "demonstrated," for example, that *Ulysses* and *Finnegan's Wake* cannot be by
the same author, and that Jane Austen's novels were not written
during the Napoleonic Wars, since she never mentions them. Hunwicke also alludes to a famous episode in the career of Msgr. Ron-
ald Knox, who once delivered a paper in which he proved, with the
methods of modern (i.e., early twentieth-century) biblical scholarship, that many of the Sherlock Holmes stories were not written by
their putative author but by an admirer whom he dubbed "Deutero-
Watson." (The notoriously credulous Sir Arthur Conan-Doyle, not
realizing that the paper was written as a satire, sent Knox a letter
to assure him that he was indeed the author of the entire *Corpus
Holmesianum*.) Unsurprisingly, the digital age has given us more
sophisticated methods of stylistic analysis than Morton had at his
disposal in the 1960s, and Hunwicke reports that Anthony Kenny
of Baliol College, Oxford, in his 1986 book *A Stylometric Study of the
New Testament*, "comprehensively torpedoed below the waterline"
several of the basic "New Testament expert" assumptions about St.
Paul. Not only does he vindicate the Pauline authorship of the two
Epistles to Timothy (the three Pastoral Epistles having generally
been considered the least Pauline of all), but also shows that the
Letter to the Hebrews "achieves a correlation with 'Paul' higher
than any other correlations in the New Testament except that
between the three Synoptic Gospels." (I am indebted to Gregory
DiPippo for the observations in this paragraph.)

why it is different in the specifically Melchizedekian-priestly and Yom-kippur-liturgical mode that it is. These foci would be interesting, indeed fascinating, to anyone biblically-minded, but they would not be particularly forceful or historically and pastorally pertinent, for anyone but these priests. The priests Paul addressed needed to be convinced, or reconvinced, that their Old Testament priesthood in the Aaronic-Levitical order had been fulfilled in their vowed obligation to the New Testament priesthood of the Melchizedekian order of Jesus Christ. They also needed to be convinced that Christ had once for all fulfilled the Yom-Kippur liturgy, and that making the grace of that liturgy, fulfilled in Christ, present and applied to the Christian faithful was their solemnly vowed, regular duty: "not forsaking our own synagogue [*episynagogein eauton*] as has become the custom of some" (Heb 10:25). The church is not opposed to the temple and synagogue; the church *is* the temple and synagogue fulfilled "outside the camp"[21] in the eucharistic sacrifice of Jesus the Messiah and High Priest of the new covenant.

Finally, this also implies that the *lex orandi* attribution of this letter to St. Paul in the lectionary tradition of both East and West transcends a naive piety handing on historical falsehood without reflection. Rather, it reveals attention to the form and content of the letter itself and transmits historical awareness of authorial complexity. Hebrews is Paul but more elegant, or, we might say now, Paul but more priestly. This tradition of Pauline authorship also respects a central teaching of St. Paul

---

[21] Israel, six centuries earlier than the letter to the Hebrews, had experienced the same historical reality: the temple and its sacrifices continued apace, but were slated soon for destruction because of hardness of heart. The glory of the temple would leave the temple, and go to those "outside the camp," the exiles in Babylon. And God sent priests to these exiles, to talk to them about not going back, and about the renewed priesthood, in a new covenant, in a new temple. I refer especially to the writings of the priest-prophets Jeremiah (1–7; 29–31) and Ezekiel (1–11, 36–37, 40–48).

himself, namely, the importance of holding fast to "the traditions." No one in the New Testament speaks more frequently, positively, forcefully, and affirmatively about acquiescence to tradition as necessary for fidelity to the Gospel, and for sanity during confusing times — until the end of time — than does St. Paul (1 Cor 11:2, 16; 15:1–7; Gal 1:8; 2:2; 2 Thes 2:15; 3:6). And no one preserved and handed on more broadly and universally the tradition that this letter was "Lectio Epistolae Beati Pauli Apostoli ad Hebraeos"[22] than the church indicated as the letter's historical and geographical source in the last sentence before the closing: "Those from Italy greet you."

This greeting forms the implicit canonical Pauline inclusion, since the corpus of letters encompassed by Paul-as-author begins with him as the Hebrew writing to the Romans (East to West), and ends with him in Rome, writing to the Hebrews (West to East). That the Eastern and Western churches retain, in their traditional liturgies, the *lex orandi* attribution of this letter to St. Paul makes the *sensus fidei* and the voice of universal tradition clear: Paul authored Hebrews.

Ironically, it was the Lectionary stemming from the work of a pope who took the name of Paul (VI) that dropped the name of Paul from the attribution of the letter to the Hebrews, though the decision came relatively late. The *Ordo Lectionum Missae* of 1969, no. 21, in the *praenotanda*, was the first to assert "today all consent" that Paul was not the author of Hebrews, and to remove the attribution to Paul. The 1981 edition, no. 48, however, removed the misleading assertion that "today all consent" while yet retaining the impersonal announcement "A reading from the letter to the Hebrews."[23] A charitable interpretation of these decisions might indicate a

---

[22] As given in the traditional Roman liturgical books, to which corresponds a correlative phrase in the Byzantine Liturgy: "The reading from the epistle of the holy apostle Paul to the Hebrews."
[23] My thanks to Matthew Hazell for these insights on the *OLM*.

remedial, pastoral condescension toward those affected
by modern skepticism to help them listen to the letter
untroubled by questions of authorship, and a simulta-
neous desire not to contradict outright the tradition of
Pauline authorship and offend those attentive to it, perhaps in an attempt to form the conditions for a happier
day when the storm is over. I am unaware of indications
that this strategy has worked.

Thus, what St. Thomas says in commenting on the
penultimate verse of the letter is essentially what faith,
reason, and tradition all have to say about the authorship
of Hebrews: "For he [Paul] wrote this epistle from Rome."

2

The Sacrifice of Christ as an Act of Vicarious Satisfaction

JOHN P. JOY

THE EPISTLE TO THE HEBREWS DWELLS at length on the high priesthood of Christ. Christ's high priesthood, like every priesthood, is intimately connected with sacrifice. To be a priest is to offer sacrifice. As the Apostle writes to the Hebrews: "Every high priest taken from among men is ordained for men in the things that appertain to God, that he may offer up gifts and sacrifices for sins" (Heb 5:1). The Council of Trent also says: "Sacrifice and priesthood are so joined together by God's foundation that each exists in every law."[1]

The high priesthood of Christ is therefore inseparable from his perfect act of sacrifice. Christ our Lord offered himself as a sacrifice upon the altar of the cross in order that we might be cleansed by his blood. He is both the high priest who offers and the spotless victim that is offered as a sacrifice for our sins. To quote again from the Letter to the Hebrews: "But Christ, taking the position of high priest of the good things to come, by a greater and more perfect tabernacle, not made with hands, that is, not of this creation: neither by the blood of goats or of calves, but by his own blood, entered once into the holies, having obtained eternal redemption" (Heb 9:11–12).

---

[1] Council of Trent, Session XXIII (1563), *On the Sacrament of Order*, 1.

So, what I shall do here, as a way of gaining some insight into the priesthood of Christ, is reflect upon his sacrifice on Calvary. And to do this, I will be contrasting the Catholic doctrine of vicarious satisfaction and the typically Protestant theory of penal substitution.

PENAL SUBSTITUTION

According to the penal substitution theory of the atonement, the death of Christ is essentially a matter of our Lord offering himself as a substitute to suffer in our place the penalty we deserved for our sins. The unrelenting justice of God demands that sin be punished. So in order to save us from our just penalty, Christ literally changes places with sinful humanity, taking upon himself the punishment for sin in order to satisfy God's justice and thus allow us to receive God's mercy instead.

In the theology of Martin Luther, this penal substitution is rooted in his doctrine of justification by faith alone.[2] The "joyous exchange" by which the merits of Christ are attributed to the sinner, so that he is reckoned as righteous despite his own unrighteousness, and therefore receives salvation as his just reward, involves a similar transfer of the demerits of the sinner to Christ, so that he is reckoned as the greatest sinner despite his own sinlessness, and therefore receives death as the punishment for sin. Luther writes: "Making a happy change with us, He took upon Him our sinful person, and gave unto us His innocent and victorious person."[3]

Similarly, John Calvin says: "Our acquittal is in this — that the guilt which made us liable to punishment was

---

[2] As Timothy George remarks, "One cannot so easily separate Luther's understanding of Christ's work on the cross from his doctrine of justification by faith." See George, "The Atonement in Martin Luther's Theology," in *The Glory of the Atonement: Biblical, Theological, and Practical Perspectives*, ed. Charles E. Hill and Frank A. James III (IVP Academic, 2004), 264.

[3] Martin Luther, *Commentary on Galatians*, ed. John Prince Fallowes, trans. Erasmus Middleton (Kregel Classics, 1978), 172.

transferred to the head of the Son of God."[4] And so: "The punishment to which we were liable was inflicted on that Just One."[5] For Calvin as for Luther, the guilt of mankind is legally imputed to Christ, whom God punishes in our stead, while the justice of Christ is similarly imputed to sinners. Penal substitution and forensic justification are two sides of the same coin.

Now there are three potential problems with this view that I want to highlight. The first is this: for all its insistence on the justice of God being fulfilled, there does not actually seem to be anything just about punishing an innocent person in place of a guilty person, even if the innocent party should offer himself willingly.[6] There is admittedly something quite attractive in seeing Christ in the role of a St. Maximilian Kolbe, voluntarily offering his own life in place of the condemned man. Much less attractive, however, is the implication that God the Father plays a part analogous to the Gestapo. If God is perfectly good and perfectly just, and if it is unjust to punish an innocent person for sins he did not commit, then the death of Christ cannot be a matter of God punishing Christ in our stead.

The second problem arises from the fact that the punishment we deserve for our sins in strict justice is not merely death, but damnation. If God's justice demands that the full penalty for sin must be paid, then merely dying upon the cross would be insufficient — Christ

---

[4] John Calvin, *Institutes of the Christian Religion*, vol. 1, trans. Henry Beveridge (T&T Clark, 1863), bk. II, 16.5.

[5] Ibid.

[6] See, for example, Eleanore Stump, *Aquinas* (Routledge, 2003), 428: "[Penal substitution (P)] seems not to emphasize God's justice but to rest on a denial of it. For all the talk of debt is really a metaphor. What (P) is in fact telling us is that any human being's sins are so great that it is a violation of justice not to punish that person with damnation. What God does in response, however, is to punish not the sinner but a perfectly innocent person instead (a person who, even on the doctrine of the Trinity, is not the same person as God the Father, who does the punishing). But how is this just?"

would also have to endure the pains of hell.[7] And in fact, this is how Calvin interprets the Apostles' Creed where it says that Christ descended into hell. He writes: "Nothing had been done if Christ had only endured corporeal death. In order to interpose between us and God's anger, and satisfy his righteous judgment, it was necessary that he should feel the weight of divine vengeance."[8] And then he goes on to say that, in addition to the bodily pain endured on the Cross, Christ "bore in his soul the tortures of condemned and ruined man."[9] In Latin the words he uses here are *damnati et perditi* (damnation and perdition). Martin Luther likewise says that Christ "really and truly offered Himself to the Father for eternal punishment on our behalf."[10]

Even some Catholic theologians — notably the late Hans Urs von Balthasar — have taken up this idea of Christ suffering the pains of hell. According to von Balthasar, Holy Saturday rather than Good Friday is at the center of the drama of redemption. While his body lay in silence in the tomb, the soul of Christ in hell suffered a horrific direct vision of death itself, somehow analogous to the beatific vision of God enjoyed by the blessed in heaven.[11] To use the scholastic system of notation, I would say this

---

[7] Ibid., 429: "[Penal substitution] claims that in his suffering and death on the cross Christ paid the full penalty for all human sin so that humans would not have to pay it; and yet it also claims that the penalty for sin is everlasting damnation. But no matter what sort of agony Christ experienced in his crucifixion, it certainly was not (and was not equivalent to) everlasting punishment, if for no other reason than that Christ's suffering came to an end."

[8] Calvin, *Institutes*, II, 16.10.

[9] Ibid.

[10] Martin Luther, *Commentary on Romans*, cited in Anthony W. Bartlett, *Cross Purposes: The Violent Grammar of Christian Atonement* (Trinity Press, 2001), 90.

[11] Hans Urs von Balthasar, *Mysterium Paschale: The Mystery of Easter*, trans. Aidan Nichols (Ignatius Press, 2005), 168–76. For a devastating critique of Balthasar's *descensus* theology, see Alyssa Lyra Pitstick, *Light in Darkness: Hans Urs von Balthasar and the Catholic Doctrine of Christ's Descent into Hell* (Eerdmans, 2007).

merits at least the theological censure "offensive to pious ears." In fact, I find it hard to see how the doctrine of a damned Christ can be anything other than heretical. The essential punishment of hell is the state of separation from God (Mt 25:41; Lk 13:27; 14:24; Rev 22:15). To say that Christ endured this seems to imply either an Arian schism between Father and Son or a Nestorian schism between the divine and human natures of Christ.

The third and final problem that I want to mention here is this: If Christ endured the full punishment for all the sins of all men, then it would be unjust for God to punish any of them, for that would be to punish the same sin twice.[12] Thus we would have to say either that all men are saved (which is the heresy of universalism) or that Christ died only for the sins of the elect (which is the heresy of limited atonement). For a Catholic, neither option is acceptable.

ST. THOMAS AQUINAS

Let us turn now to St. Thomas Aquinas and his understanding of the sacrifice of Christ as an act of vicarious satisfaction. Here I want to consider four points: First, St. Thomas's account of sacrifice in general; secondly, St. Thomas's account of satisfaction in general; thirdly, the death of Christ as a sacrifice that satisfies for sins. And then finally, the application of the fruits of his passion to individual men and women.

Sacrifice as an Act of Justice

According to St. Thomas, offering sacrifice to God is essentially a matter of justice. More precisely, the act of

---

[12] Stump, *Aquinas*, 429: "[Penal substitution] maintains that Christ pays the penalty for all sin in full so that humans do not have to do so. But it is a fundamental Christian doctrine that God justly condemns some people to everlasting punishment in hell. If Christ has paid the penalty for sin completely, how is God just in demanding that some people pay the penalty again?"

sacrifice is an act of the virtue of religion, which is connected to justice. Justice in general is the virtue whereby
one gives to each what is due to him; religion is the virtue
of giving to God what is due to him. And that which
man owes to God as his Creator and sovereign Lord is
reverence and honor, acknowledging God's surpassing
excellence and our complete dependence on him.[13]

St. Thomas distinguishes between interior and exterior
acts of the virtue of religion. The principal acts of religion are the interior acts of prayer and devotion. Prayer
is the intellect's act of submission to God; devotion is
the act of the will offering itself in subjection to God.[14]
The worship of God is thus primarily an inward spiritual
matter. But there are also exterior acts of religion. And
this is necessary on account of human nature, for we are
bodily as well as spiritual creatures, and the human mind
is led by visible signs to the contemplation of invisible
things.[15] Thus man must subject to God not only his soul,
but also his body and even his external possessions. And

---

[13] See St. Thomas Aquinas, *Summa theologiae* [henceforth: *ST*]
II-II, q. 81, on the virtue of religion in itself. All citations of the
Summa theologiae are taken from the translation of the Fathers of
the English Dominican Province (Benzinger, 1947).
[14] See *ST* II-II, qq. 82–83, on devotion and on prayer.
[15] See *ST* II-II, q. 81, a. 7: "We pay God honor and reverence, not
for His sake (because He is of Himself full of glory to which no
creature can add anything), but for our own sake, because by the
very fact that we revere and honor God, our mind is subjected to
Him; wherein its perfection consists, since a thing is perfected by
being subjected to its superior, for instance the body is perfected
by being quickened by the soul, and the air by being enlightened by the sun. Now the human mind, in order to be united to
God, needs to be guided by the sensible world, since 'invisible
things… are clearly seen, being understood by the things that are
made,' as the Apostle says (Rm. 1:20). Wherefore in the Divine
worship it is necessary to make use of corporeal things, that man's
mind may be aroused thereby, as by signs, to the spiritual acts by
means of which he is united to God. Therefore the internal acts
of religion take precedence of the others and belong to religion
essentially, while its external acts are secondary, and subordinate
to the internal acts."

the interior subjection of will and intellect are fittingly expressed through the physical acts of reverence (such as prostrations, genuflections, making the sign of the Cross, etc.) and the offering of sacrifices.[16]

As a general definition of sacrifice we could say, therefore, that a sacrifice is the external act of offering some good to God as an expression of the internal reverence and honor that is due to him as our Creator and Lord.[17] The animal sacrifices of the Old Testament were not offered as though God needed to eat the flesh of cattle or drink the blood of goats, as the psalms and the prophets were constantly reminding the people of Israel; they were meant to be signs of interior devotion. As St. Augustine says: "The visible sacrifice is the sacrament or sacred sign of the invisible sacrifice."[18] The exterior acts of sacrifice are secondary and subordinate to the interior acts, but

---

[16] See *ST* II-II, qq. 84–85.

[17] See *ST* II-II, q. 85, a. 1: "Natural reason tells man that he is subject to a higher being, on account of the defects which he perceives in himself, and in which he needs help and direction from someone above him: and whatever this superior being may be, it is known to all under the name of God. Now just as in natural things the lower are naturally subject to the higher, so too it is a dictate of natural reason in accordance with man's natural inclination that he should tender submission and honor, according to his mode, to that which is above man. Now the mode befitting to man is that he should employ sensible signs in order to signify anything, because he derives his knowledge from sensibles. Hence it is a dictate of natural reason that man should use certain sensibles, by offering them to God in sign of the subjection and honor due to Him, like those who make certain offerings to their lord in recognition of his authority. Now this is what we mean by a sacrifice, and consequently the offering of sacrifice is of the natural law."

[18] See *ST* II-II, q. 81, a. 7, ad 2: "These external things are offered to God, not as though He stood in need of them, according to Ps. 49:13, 'Shall I eat the flesh of bullocks? or shall I drink the blood of goats?' but as signs of the internal and spiritual works, which are of themselves acceptable to God. Hence Augustine says (*De Civ. Dei* x, 5): 'The visible sacrifice is the sacrament or sacred sign of the invisible sacrifice.'"

they are necessary. Man is not a pure spirit; his bodily
nature requires that his interior acts find completion in
outward expression. At the same time, the mind of man
is led from exterior things to interior things. Thus the
exterior sacrifice both leads to and proceeds from the
interior sacrifice. By offering outward sacrifices man is
led to inward devotion and prayer, and the devout soul
in turn seeks to express its devotion in sensible signs
and actions.

Satisfaction as an Act of Justice

We come now to the second point: satisfaction as an
act of justice. Reverence and honor are due to God on
account of his majesty, and hence sacrifice as an act of
worship belongs to the law of nature. But something
more is due to God on account of sin. And so after the
fall, sacrifice takes on the additional aspect of satisfaction for sin.

If we think first about ordinary human affairs, satisfaction and punishment are two distinct ways in which the
order of justice may be restored after an injustice has been
committed.[19] Let us say, for example, that in a moment

---

[19] Aquinas follows St. Anselm in distinguishing between punishment and satisfaction as alternative means of restoring justice: "If,
however, sin is neither paid for nor punished, then it is subject
to no law" (St. Anselm, *Cur Deus Homo*, I, 12); "Does it seem
to you that he [God] wholly preserves it [his honor], if he thus
permits himself to be robbed, such that neither is he repaid nor
does he punish the thief?... It is necessary, therefore, that either
the stolen honor be repaid or punishment follow" (ibid., I, 13).
See also Rik van Nieuwenhove, "'Bearing the Marks of Christ's
Passion': Aquinas' Soteriology," in *The Theology of Thomas Aquinas*,
ed. Rik van Nieuwenhove and Joseph Wawrykow (University of
Notre Dame Press, 2005), 288: "Whereas 'satisfaction' is popularly
misunderstood in terms of meeting the demands of vindictive
justice (Christ is being punished on our behalf), for Anselm
satisfaction rules out punishment: *aut poena aut satisfactio.*" Unlike
Anselm, however, Aquinas holds that it would not have been
contrary to justice for God to forgive sins without satisfaction
(*ST* III, q. 46, a. 2, ad 3).

of anger I deliberately smashed one of Chris's favorite cups. Perhaps even his Birra Nursia chalice. The order of justice has been broken, not to mention, I suspect, our friendship. But justice can be restored here in two different ways. One option would be for Chris to smash something of mine. This would be a fitting punishment and the equality of justice would be restored. But not, I think, our friendship. The other option would be for me to give Chris something that he would value as much as or more than the original cup as compensation.

Justice is a matter of giving what is due and justice is restored in either case, but with several important differences: in the case of punishment, the guilty party passively receives the penalty that he deserves, and this is an evil inflicted upon him against his will; in satisfaction, the guilty party actively gives what is due to the one he has injured, and this compensation is something good offered voluntarily. Punishment is an act of vengeance inflicted upon the sinner; satisfaction is an act of penance performed by the sinner. Justice is restored in either case; but friendship is restored only by satisfaction.

Another crucial difference is this: it would be completely unjust for Chris to inflict a punishment on someone else instead of me — to smash Daniel's favorite cup, for example. But there is nothing contrary to justice if a third party steps in to purchase a new cup for Chris on my behalf, perhaps knowing that for some reason I cannot do so myself. Punishment is not transferable, so to speak, but satisfaction is.[20] This is why the death

---

[20] See *ST* I-II, q. 87, a. 7: "As already stated, punishment can be considered in two ways — simply, and as being satisfactory. A satisfactory punishment is, in a way, voluntary. And since those who differ as to the debt of punishment, may be one in will by the union of love, it happens that one who has not sinned, bears willingly the punishment for another: thus even in human affairs we see men take the debts of another upon themselves. If, however, we speak of punishment simply, in respect of its being something penal, it has always a relation to a sin in the one punished."

of Christ understood as a punishment inflicted by God the Father on Christ in our place would be contrary to justice; but this would not be true of the death of Christ understood as a satisfaction voluntarily offered by him to the Father on our behalf.

Now, although satisfaction is distinct from punishment, it is still fitting that there should be something penal about it, both in order to correct the past sin and to prevent future sins. I am less likely to go about smashing people's things if I see that it costs something to make things right. But the degree of pain involved in making satisfaction does not matter nearly so much as the degree of charity with which it is made. This is because satisfaction aims not only at the restoration of justice but even more at the reconciliation of friendship. A lesser gift offered out of a greater love is more acceptable than a great gift offered without love.[21]

A complete description of satisfaction, therefore, includes three parts: first and formally, satisfaction is an act of justice that gives to the injured party what is due to him in compensation for a prior offense; secondly, the offering should be materially painful to the one making satisfaction; and thirdly, it should be motivated by charity, from which it has its power of restoring friendship in addition to justice. A sacrifice offered to God as a satisfaction for sin, therefore, would have to compensate for sin by offering God something good enough to counterbalance the evil of sin; it would have to deprive

---

[21] See *ST* III, q. 14, a. 1, ad 1: "The penalties one suffers for another's sin are the matter, as it were, of the satisfaction for that sin; but the principle is the habit of soul, whereby one is inclined to wish to satisfy for another, and from which the satisfaction has its efficacy, for satisfaction would not be efficacious unless it proceeded from charity, as will be explained. Hence, it behooved the soul of Christ to be perfect as regards the habit of knowledge and virtue, in order to have the power of satisfying; but His body was subject to infirmities, that the matter of satisfaction should not be wanting."

the one offering it of some good; and it would have to be offered out of charity. The difficulty was that mankind had nothing to offer to God sufficient to counterbalance the offence of sin; and the human race fallen from grace lacked the charity that would make such a gift efficacious.

The Death of Christ as a Satisfactory Sacrifice

And so we come next to consider the death of Christ as a sacrifice that accomplishes the necessary satisfaction for sin. In question 48, articles 2 and 3, St. Thomas considers the passion of Christ as the cause of our salvation by way of satisfaction and by way of sacrifice, respectively.

The death of Christ was indeed a sacrifice since it was "something done for that honor which is properly due to God, in order to appease Him," and it was "most acceptable to God as coming from charity."[22] And Christ's death was also an act of satisfaction. As St. Thomas writes:

> He properly atones for an offense who offers something which the offended one loves equally, or even more than he detested the offense. But by suffering out of love and obedience, Christ gave more to God than was required to compensate for the offense of the whole human race. First of all, because of the exceeding charity from which He suffered; secondly, on account of the dignity of His life which He laid down in atonement, for it was the life of one who was God and man; thirdly, on account of the extent of the Passion, and the greatness of the grief endured,

---

[22] See *ST* III, q. 48, a. 3: "A sacrifice properly so called is something done for that honor which is properly due to God, in order to appease Him: and hence it is that Augustine says (*De Civ. Dei* x): 'A true sacrifice is every good work done in order that we may cling to God in holy fellowship, yet referred to that consummation of happiness wherein we can be truly blessed.' But, as is added in the same place, 'Christ offered Himself up for us in the Passion': and this voluntary enduring of the Passion was most acceptable to God, as coming from charity. Therefore it is manifest that Christ's Passion was a true sacrifice."

as stated above. And therefore Christ's Passion
was not only a sufficient but a superabundant
atonement for the sins of the human race.[23]

After the fall of Adam, the human race had no adequate
means of making satisfaction for the infinite debt of sin.
But in the death of Christ we find everything necessary for satisfaction in superabundant measure. The pain
endured by Christ in His suffering and death was more
than enough to provide the raw material of satisfaction.
The value of the good offered, which was the infinitely
precious life of the incarnate Son of God, was more than
enough to counterbalance the offense of sin; and the perfect love with which Christ voluntarily offered his life was
more than enough to reconcile God to man in friendship.

This leads us to another crucial difference between the
Protestant theory of penal substitution and the Catholic
doctrine of vicarious satisfaction. According to Luther
and Calvin, it is the punishment endured by Christ that
is placed in the balance against the infinite gravity of sin,
which leads, as we have seen, to the idea that Christ must
have experienced the full punishment of hell, which is
separation from God. For St. Thomas, on the other hand,
it is much more the value of the life offered and the
degree of charity with which it is offered that are placed
in the balance. From this point of view there is no reason
to suppose that Christ must have endured the punishment
of hell (even if it were not heretical to say so).[24]

---

[23] *ST* III, q. 48, a. 2.

[24] In fact, as it says in the *Adoro te devote*, attributed to St. Thomas,
even one drop of Christ's most precious blood would have been
enough to satisfy for all the sins of all men: *Pie Pelicane, Jesu Domine,
/ Me immundum munda tuo sanguine: / Cujus una stilla salvum facere,
/ Totum mundum quit ab omni scelere.* See also Pope Clement VI,
Bull *Unigenitus Dei* (27 Jan. 1343): "Immolated on the altar of the
Cross though he was innocent, he shed not merely a drop of
blood — although this would have sufficed for the redemption of
the whole human race because of the union with the Word — but
a copious flood, like a stream."

Application of the Fruits of Christ's Passion

In itself the sacrifice of Christ is sufficient to satisfy for the sins of all men, but the fruits of Christ's passion are applied only to those who are united to him by faith and charity.[25] Through baptism we are conformed to Christ and made members of his body, the Church, and thus constitute, as it were, one mystical person so that the satisfaction offered by the head belongs to all the faithful as members of the same body.[26] Aquinas compares this to a case in which a man uses his hands to make up for a sin committed with his feet.[27] Saint Thomas's complete vision of salvation through incorporation into Christ places his understanding of the vicarious nature of Christ's passion in stark contrast to the Lutheran idea of substitution. The persons of Christ and the sinner are not exchanged, but united.[28] Christ on the cross did not

---

[25] *ST* III, q. 49, a. 1, ad 5: "Christ's Passion is applied to us even through faith, that we may share in its fruits, according to Rm. 3:25: 'Whom God hath proposed to be a propitiation, through faith in His blood.' But the faith through which we are cleansed from sin is not 'lifeless faith,' which can exist even with sin, but 'faith living' through charity; that thus Christ's Passion may be applied to us, not only as to our minds, but also as to our hearts. And even in this way sins are forgiven through the power of the Passion of Christ."

[26] *ST* III, q. 48, a. 2, ad 1: "The head and members are as one mystic person; and therefore Christ's satisfaction belongs to all the faithful as being His members. Also, in so far as any two men are one in charity, the one can atone for the other as shall be shown later."

[27] *ST* III, q. 49, a. 1: "For since He is our head, then, by the Passion which He endured from love and obedience, He delivered us as His members from our sins, as by the price of His Passion: in the same way as if a man by the good industry of his hands were to redeem himself from a sin committed with his feet. For, just as the natural body is one though made up of diverse members, so the whole Church, Christ's mystic body, is reckoned as one person with its head, which is Christ."

[28] See Nieuwenhove, "Bearing the Marks of Christ's Passion," 290: "This idea of incorporation in Christ—becoming part of the body of Christ—is crucial to preclude a misunderstanding of Aquinas' soteriology in transactional or even substitutional terms."

do something so that sinners would not have to; he did something that sinners could not do, so that through him, with him, and in him, they would be able to do it. Rather than simply doing it for us, God chose to grant us the great dignity of participating in our own redemption.

Far from excusing man from his duties toward God in justice, Christ's sacrifice actually enables man finally to fulfill them. Having once offered up his perfect sacrifice to the Father, Christ placed it into the hands of the Church to be offered daily by her priests, so that men might finally be able to offer pleasing worship to God and make satisfaction for the sins that they daily commit. As a sacrament, the Eucharist benefits only those who receive it, provided that they receive it worthily. As a sacrifice, it benefits all those who offer it and all those for whom it is offered. By the offering of the eucharistic sacrifice, man first fulfills the requirements of justice. By receiving the eucharistic sacrament, he is then perfected in union with Christ by charity. Justice is perfected by charity, but charity presupposes justice and man is bound in justice to offer sacrifice to God. As a sacrifice the Eucharist first feeds the souls of those who hunger and thirst for justice; as a sacrament it then feeds them with the bread of angels.

3

How Is the Mass a Sacrifice?

REV. THOMAS CREAN, O.P.

ONE OF THE MAIN THEMES OF THE *EPIS-tle to the Hebrews* is how the many Old Testament sacrifices have been replaced by the one sacrifice of Christ. For example, Heb. 9:28 says: "Christ was offered once to exhaust/bear the sins of many." Yet at the same time we have a sacrifice in the liturgy of the New Testament, namely the Mass. As a matter of fact, I believe that there are allusions to this within Hebrews itself, most obviously in the statement of Heb. 13:10: "We have an altar." However, this talk will not directly consider the letter to the Hebrews, but simply consider the question: "In what sense is the Mass a sacrifice?"

I shall work through the question systematically, relying in particular on the magisterium of Church. When we've gone as far as we can by means the magisterium, we'll look at various suggestions by different theologians about how to go further.

Which are the key magisterial texts? The most important one is the *Decree on the most holy sacrifice of the Mass*, promulgated in Session 22 of the Council of Trent, on September 17, 1562. Among more recent documents one should note in particular *Mirae caritatis*, an encyclical of Leo XIII from 1902; *Mediator Dei*, Pius XII's encyclical on the liturgy from 1947; the *Catechism of the Catholic Church*, paragraphs 1362–1372; and John Paul II's encyclical from 2003, *Ecclesia de Eucharistia*, especially paragraphs 12 and 13.

IN THE MASS, A TRUE AND PROPER SACRIFICE IS OFFERED TO GOD

The decree of the Council of Trent is so important that I'll quote it at some length. Session 22, chapter 1 says this:

> He, our Lord and God, was once and for all to offer Himself to God the Father by His death on the altar of the Cross to accomplish there an everlasting redemption. But because His priesthood was not to end with His death, at the Last Supper, "on the night when he was betrayed," in order to leave to His beloved Spouse the Church a visible sacrifice, such as the nature of man requires, by which the bloody sacrifice that He was once for all to accomplish on the Cross would be represented [*repraesentaretur*] and its memory perpetuated until the end of the world, and also its saving power applied for the forgiveness of the sins that we daily commit—declaring Himself a priest forever according to the order of Melchisedek, He offered His body and blood under the appearance of bread and wine to God the Father, and under the same signs, gave them to partake of to the disciples (whom He then established as priests of the New Covenant) and ordered them and their successors in the priesthood to offer, saying, "Do this in remembrance of me," as the Catholic Church has always understood and taught. For Christ having celebrated the ancient Pasch, which the multitude of the sons of Israel immolated in memory of the exodus from Egypt, instituted a new Pasch, Himself, to be offered by the Church through priests under visible signs in memory of His passing from this world to the Father, when by the shedding of His blood, He redeemed us and delivered us from the dominion of darkness and transferred us to His kingdom.

This is a very rich passage. For the moment, I'll just draw your attention to the teaching that the Mass is a visible sacrifice, as the nature of man requires, that Christ offered it at Last Supper, and that He established a priesthood to do the same.

We should note also some of the "canons," that is, definitions, with which the decree concludes. Canon 1 says: "If anyone says that in the Mass, a true and proper sacrifice (*verum ac proprium sacrificium*) is not offered to God, or that the offering consists merely in the fact that Christ is given to us to eat, let him be anathema." Canon 3 says: "If anyone says that the sacrifice of the Mass is merely one of praise and thanksgiving, or that it is a simple commemoration (*nuda commemoratio*) of the sacrifice accomplished on the Cross, but not a propitiatory sacrifice, or that it benefits only those who communicate; and that it should not be offered for the living and the dead, for sins, punishments, satisfaction, and other necessities, let him be anathema."

The word "propitiatory" is important. Protestants, then as now, were willing to speak of a Eucharistic sacrifice in a broad sense, that is, as an offering of praise and thanksgiving to God. But Trent defined that since a true and proper sacrifice is offered to God by the Mass, it is also propitiatory; that is, it appeases God's justice. Incidentally, the word "propitiatory" was omitted from the first, provisional version of the *Catechism of the Catholic Church*, in 1992; happily, it was inserted into the official Latin edition published five years later.

However, this still leaves us with the question, why exactly is the Mass a sacrifice? We can see, at least to some extent, why our Lord's death on the Cross is a sacrifice. It was a free offering of His life to God on behalf of mankind. But why do we call the Mass a sacrifice? The real presence of Christ is not enough to explain it, since that remains wherever the Blessed Sacrament is reserved, and we don't speak of the "sacrifice of the tabernacle" as we speak of the sacrifice of the altar.

THERE IS A CLOSE RELATIONSHIP BETWEEN
THE SACRIFICE OF THE CROSS AND MASS

This brings us to the second point. There is a close relationship between the Sacrifice of the Cross and the Holy Mass. We have seen that Trent emphasized this point. It taught that by the Mass, the Cross is represented, and so its memory is perpetuated, and that the saving power of the Cross is applied for the remission of the sins that we daily commit. This last statement does not mean that going to Mass remits sin directly, like receiving the sacrament of penance, but rather that from the Mass we receive the grace to be sorry for these sins, and also, as canon 3 says, the debt of punishment or satisfaction due because of past, forgiven sins is lessened. Chapter 2 of the Tridentine decree likewise emphasizes the unity between the Sacrifice of the Cross and that of the Mass: "The victim is one and the same; the same now offers Himself through the ministry of priests who then offered Himself on the Cross; only the manner of offering (*offerendi ratio*) is different." How exactly are they different? Trent says: on the Cross, our Lord offered Himself "in a bloody manner" (*cruente*), here He is offered (*immolatur*) in an unbloody way (*incruente*), since He does not die again.

Later magisterial texts have used a variety of words to attempt to express this relationship between the Sacrifice of Calvary and that of the altar. In *Mirae caritatis*, Leo XIII calls the Mass a mystical renewal, *renovatio*, of the Cross: "[The Eucharist] is not a mere commemoration, but a true and wondrous, though unbloody and mystical renewal of His death."[1] The same pope, writing to the bishops of Scotland, used the verb *continuo* to describe the relationship:

---

[1] *Acta Apostolicae Sedis* [henceforth: *AAS*] 34:653: "... Eucharistia, quae mortis ipsius non inanis quaedam nudaque commemoratio, sed vera et mirabilis, quamquam incruenta et mystica, renovatio est."

> That sacrifice [of the Cross] is continued by the
> Eucharistic sacrifice ... For since religion must
> at all times be accompanied by some sacrificial
> rite, it was the divine purpose of our Redeemer
> that the sacrifice once only consummated on the
> Cross, should become perpetual and everlasting.[2]

Pius XI, in his encyclical *Miserentissimus Redemptor*, also uses the term *renovare*, to describe the relationship, teaching that the bloody sacrifice of the Cross "is renewed without any interruption upon our altars in an unbloody way."[3]

Pius XII, in *Mediator Dei*, speaks of the Mass as "a true and proper act of sacrificing" (*vera ac propria sacrificatio*), and he uses the verbs *representare* and *innovare* to express its relation to the Cross. *Representare* seems here, as in Trent, to have its ordinary meaning, "to represent"; *innovare* seems to mean the same as *renovare*, though perhaps better avoids the suggestion that the Mass is a simple repetition of the Cross.[4]

The Catechism of the Catholic Church, in paragraph 1366, like Trent and Pius XII, uses the verb *repraesentare*, but seems to wish to give it a stronger sense: "The Eucharist is therefore a sacrifice because it *represents* (makes present) the sacrifice of the Cross."[5] The parenthesis, which is of course present in the text and not added by me, warns us not to suppose that "representation" in the usual sense of the word is a full explanation of the relation between the two forms of Christ's sacrifice; however, it does not explain what is meant by "makes present."

Finally, St. John Paul II, in *Ecclesia de Eucharistia* says this:

> The Mass makes present the Sacrifice of the
> Cross, it is not added to it, nor does it multiply

---

[2] *AAS* 31:12: "Illud sacrificium [Crucis] sacrificio eucharistico continuatur..."

[3] *AAS* 20:170: "...incruente modo renovatur."

[4] *AAS* 39:548, 580.

[5] "Eucharistia est igitur sacrificium quia Sacrificium crucis *repraesentat* (praesens reddit)."

it. What is repeated is the memorial celebration
and demonstration of the Cross, whereby the
unique and perpetually redemptive sacrifice of
Christ shows itself as always efficacious in time.
In virtue of its relation with the sacrifice of Gol-
gotha, the Eucharist is a sacrifice in the proper
sense of the word.[6]

To sum up this section: the popes teach that Holy
Mass renews, continues, and makes present the sacrifice
of the Cross, and that it is the means by which the Cross
continually manifests its power. However, we still want
to understand *how* it does these things. In particular, why
does the way in which it does these things allow us to
say the Mass is *itself* a true and proper sacrifice? As a first
step to answering this, let us consider more closely the
Mass as a commemoration or memorial of the Cross.

MASS IS AN OBJECTIVE MEMORIAL OF THE CROSS

The Mass is an objective memorial of the sacrifice of
the Cross. This is the first thing that the Tridentine decree
teaches. We say "objective," to indicate that the Mass
is such a memorial in itself, independently of whether
anyone is actually thinking about the Cross during a
given offering of the Mass. St. Paul expresses this idea
of objective memorial in 1 Cor. 11: "As often as you shall
eat this bread, and drink the chalice, you shall show
(καταγγέλλετε) the death of the Lord, until he comes." The
Greek word translated here as "you shall show" could also
be translated as "you announce, proclaim, declare," but
hardly as "you remember." It is the act itself of offering
Mass that constitutes the memorial, not the thoughts

---

[6] Pope John Paul II, *Ecclesia de Eucharistia*, 12–13: "Sacrificium
Crucis presens efficit Missa, non illi adiungitur neque id mul-
tiplicat. Quod repetitur est memorialis celebratio, memorialis
demonstratio ipsius, unde unicum et pstremum redimens Christi
sacrificium sese in tempore semper efficax praestat.... Virtute
huius suae necessitudines cum Gologthae sacrificio Eucharistia
sensu proprio sacrificium est."

of those present. The Mass would still be an objective memorial of Christ's sacrifice on the Cross, even if no one present were thinking about the Cross.

Note, incidentally, that St. Paul doesn't say that whenever Mass is said in Corinth, they show the death and resurrection of Christ, but simply, His death. It has become rather common in recent years to speak of the Mass as a commemoration of the death and resurrection of Christ, but this is a loose way of speaking. The phrase appears in the constitution *Sacrosanctum Concilium* of Vatican II, paragraph 47, and from there entered into paragraph 2 of the *General Instruction* at the start of the Missal of Paul VI. The problem with this phrase is not that it is false, but that it seems misleadingly to equate the sense in which the Mass is a memorial of the death of our Lord, as St. Paul says, with a quite different sense in which it could be called a memorial of His Resurrection. It is a commemoration of the former objectively, simply in virtue of what is done at Mass. It can be a commemoration of the latter, but subjectively, insofar as it prompts us to think about the resurrection. In any case, I have not been able to trace the phrase about the Mass as a memorial of the death and resurrection of Christ to any authoritative document before Vatican II. *Ecclesia de Eucharistia* returns to the traditional language in paragraph 12; quoting *Mediator Dei*, it describes Mass as a "commemorative representation" simply of the Cross.

HOW IS THE MASS AN OBJECTIVE MEMORIAL OF THE CROSS?

Historically, this has been a disputed question. St. Thomas Aquinas does not address this question as directly as some later writers, but touches on it rather in passing. In the *Summa Theologiae*, 3a 76 a. 2 ad 1, replying to the objection that there would be no need to have both Eucharistic species if the whole Christ is present under each, he says: "This serves to represent the passion of

Christ, in which the blood was poured out separately from His body." In the ad 2, likewise, he explains the separate consecrations of the body and blood in virtue of the sacrament's being a memorial of the passion. However, in q. 74, a. 1, he speaks of the separate *reception* of the Eucharistic species as representing the passion.

Some theologians, who have considered the question expressly, have proposed that communion is essential for Mass to be a memorial of Cross. But there have been two very different accounts of this. An older theory, put forward by St. Robert Bellarmine and St. Alphonsus Liguori, held that destruction was essential to the idea of sacrifice. On the Cross, Christ's human life was destroyed. Therefore, they suggested, since Holy Communion destroys the sacramental species, Communion is an essential element in the Mass, considered precisely as a memorial of the Cross. This theory takes in a very literal way the text from St. Paul quoted above, since on this account it is precisely the "eating and drinking" that proclaims "the death of the Lord." However, the liturgy never speaks of communion as a means of placating God, but as means to be sanctified by Him as having already been placated.

A much more modern account about how Communion is essential to the Mass as a memorial of the Cross emphasizes the fact that Christ's death was an act of love for mankind. Therefore, since Holy Communion is a fraternal banquet, it commemorates the love of Christ, and in this sense causes the Mass to be a memorial of His sacrificial death. This account forgets, however, that, as *Ecclesia de Eucharistia* 13 says, the offering which Christ made of Himself on the Cross was first of all an offering to His Father. Therefore, for the Mass to be a memorial of the sacrifice of the Cross, it must represent not just Christ's love for mankind, but primarily His offering of Himself to God.

Others have argued that the Mass principally commemorates Christ's death in virtue of the verbal reference to that death after the consecration (traditionally, in the

Roman rite, by the prayer *Unde et memores*), or else by the fraction of the host, representing the "breaking" of Christ's body upon the Cross. However, the idea that the fraction is by itself the key representative part of the Mass seems implausible, while the suggestion that the verbal commemoration of Christ's death in the anaphora is the essential part does not allow us to explain why the Mass is traditionally called a commemoration of the death and not of the resurrection or ascension, since both these things are also mentioned in the anaphora (and the second coming also, in the Byzantine rite).

In any case, while this had been historically an open question, Catholic theologians cannot now consider it so, since an authoritative statement about it was made in Pius XII's encyclical *Mediator Dei.* He wrote as follows:

> By the transubstantiation of the bread into the Body of Christ and of the wine into His Blood, the Eucharistic appearances, under which the body and blood are present, represent the bloody separation of the body and blood. Therefore, the commemorative demonstration (*memorialis demonstratio*) of His death which really took place on Calvary, is repeated in all the sacrifices of the altar, insofar as Christ Jesus is represented and shown in a state of victimhood by these distinct tokens of His death.[7]

In other words, not only is our Lord is really present, but His death is represented by the twofold consecration of the body and the blood, representing the physical separation on the Cross. Pius XII made no reference to Holy Communion in regard to the representative character of the Mass, and so the "Bellarminian" thesis on this point may be regarded as having been authoritatively set aside. Again, in opposition to the view that Holy Communion insofar as it is a fraternal banquet represents the sacrifice of the Cross, Pius XII repudiates the idea of common

---

[7] *AAS* 39:548s.

communion as the highpoint, *culmen*, of the Mass.[8]

This presents the Mass as a kind of picture of Calvary. And St. Thomas uses this very term in explaining why we talk of Christ as being "immolated" in the Mass. In the *Summa Theologiae*, 3a, 83, 1, he writes:

> As Augustine says, "pictures are generally called by the names of the things of which they are pictures: for example, we look at a painting or a fresco and say, that is Cicero, that is Sallust." And the celebration of his sacrament is a kind of picture (*imago est quaedam*) that represents the passion of Christ, which is a true immolation.

We can also note here, with theologians such as Lessius and Billuart, that what represents the passion of Christ is not simply the fact that the separated species of bread and wine represent the separation of His body and blood on the Cross, but also the fact that the "sacramental separation" of His body and blood at Mass represents their physical separation in the Cross. Sacramental separation means that our Lord's body, and not His blood, is present under the appearances of bread strictly in virtue of the transubstantiation, that is, as the terminus of the conversion of the bread (although His blood is present there also, not in virtue of the transubstantiation, but "by virtue of concomitance," that is, because His body comes to exist on the altar with the same properties that it has in heaven, including the property of being united to His blood, soul and divinity). Likewise, His precious blood, and not His body, is present under the appearances of wine strictly in virtue of the transubstantiation, that is, as the terminus of the conversion of the wine (although His body is present there also, not in virtue of the transubstantiation, but "by virtue of concomitance," that is, because His blood comes to exist on the altar with the same properties that it has in heaven, including the property of being united to His body, soul and divinity).

---

[8] *AAS* 39:563.

It is in this sense that Christ's body and blood are said to be sacramentally or mystically separated on the altar, and this separation represents their physical separation in the Passion. The Mass is therefore a portrait of the Passion, designed by God and not by men, a portrait that is offered both to the senses, through the Eucharistic species, and to the intelligence enlightened by faith, through the sacramental separation of our Lord's body and blood.

HOW IS THE MASS A TRUE AND PROPER SACRIFICE?

So far we have considered in what way the Mass is an objective memorial of the Passion. We can see how it is such a memorial in a way that is far more profound than even the most beautiful or moving painting or sculpture of the Crucifixion. It is designed by God, not by man, and the passion is represented not by paint or by wood but by the Eucharistic species themselves which contain the true body and blood of our Lord, and by that true body and blood, insofar as they are sacramentally or mystically separated. One might argue that this gives us a sufficient explanation of why the Mass is itself called a "true and proper sacrifice," *verum ac proprium sacrificium.* Yet we still remain within the order of representation. To use the terminology of some authors, we could say that so far we have explained why the Mass is called a sacrifice relatively, and called a sacrifice in this way far more perfectly than any picture or sculpture, but that we have still not quite explained why it is called one absolutely. These two questions are doubtless very closely related, but they are not, formally speaking, the same question.

It seems that the magisterial texts don't answer this question directly. They are content to say that the Mass is a memorial of the Cross; that it is not a bare or empty memorial, but one which renews or continues or makes present the sacrifice of the Cross; and that it is itself a true sacrifice. They leave it to theologians to discuss how precisely the Mass does these things, and precisely what connection these things have to the fact that it is itself a true sacrifice.

The theologians have come up with a confusing array of accounts of the matter. The *Sacrae Theologiae Summa*, produced by Spanish Jesuits in the 1950s, and an invaluable resource for learning the state of the question on any given theological topic, distinguishes ten different theories, among which they note three main tendencies. I am not going to describe all the theories, but I shall explain what they mean by the three tendencies.

In order to do this, we should consider a question that you may think is rather overdue: what is a sacrifice? St. Thomas draws a key distinction between a sacrifice on the one hand and an offering or oblation on the other:

> Sacrifices, properly speaking, are said to exist when something happens to the things that are offered to God (*circa res Deo oblatas aliquid fit*), for example when animals are killed, or bread is broken and blessed and eaten. And the very name indicates this, since "sacrifice" is used to say that a man makes something sacred (*facit sacrum*). An oblation is said to be when something is offered to God, even if nothing happens to is (*nihil circa ipsum fiat*), as money or loaves are said to be offered on an altar, even though nothing happens to them. And so, every sacrifice is an offering, but not every offering is a sacrifice.[9]

We may note that St. Thomas does not make destruction the essential mark of a sacrifice. It is necessary that something be done to that which is offered to God, and that the very offering should consist in the doing of that something. But it is not necessary that a thing be destroyed in order for us to say that it is sacrificed.

(Here we may also take note of a third term, in addition to oblation and sacrifice, namely "immolation." The

---

[9] Thomas Aquinas, *ST* II-II, q. 85, a. 3, ad 3. The title of the question is "Whether the offering of sacrifice is a special act of religion?"

Latin term *immolatio* seems to be used to mean the sacrifice of a sentient being, as opposed to a vegetable or mineral sacrifice. So immolation is a species of sacrifice, as sacrifice is a species of offering, and so also the question of how the Mass is a sacrifice will at the same time answer the question of how it is an immolation.)

This distinction of oblation and sacrifice allows us, with the Spanish Jesuits, to divide the theories of the sacrificial nature of Mass into three main categories. Our question is how the Mass is a proper sacrifice; and naturally, this question must be asked by making reference to the Cross. Accordingly, the first set of theories argue that in relation to the Cross, there is neither a new offering nor a new sacrifice at Holy Mass. The second group argues that the Mass contains a new offering but not a new sacrifice. The third group argues that the Mass is both a new offering and a new sacrifice.

The first position, then, is that the Mass, properly speaking, involves neither a new offering or nor a new sacrifice. We can distinguish two main forms of this view. The earlier form emphasizes Christ's one act of offering of Himself to the Father, an act which, as we learn from the letter to the Hebrews, began at the moment of the incarnation. This same act continued throughout His life, was demonstrated most expressly at His death, and remains in heaven. Through the consecration, it comes to be present on the altar, since Christ is there. Therefore, we can speak of the Mass as a sacrifice. This account of the Mass is associated with seventeenth-century Oratorian Charles de Condren. In the twentieth century, it was promoted by Marius Lepin.

This account certainly contains an important truth: Christ's inward act of self-offering, motivated by charity and religion, is essential to the power of the Mass, that is, to the fruits that derive therefrom. Some authors therefore speak of this inward act as the "soul of the Mass." But is this act of Christ's will sufficient to explain why Mass is a sacrifice? One difficulty is that it does not explain why the

Mass would be specifically a renewal of Cross, rather than of, say, the fast in the desert or the hidden life or the heavenly life. Also, would we not have to say on this account that a sacrifice continues as long as the real presence?

The other version of this first tendency is rather different. Some authors assert that the sacrifice of the Mass is *numerically* the same as that of the cross. This is part of a wider theological tendency to assert that when the sacred liturgy is performed, the events of Christ's life come to be mysteriously present. It is a tendency associated with a school of German Benedictines from the early twentieth century, especially Odo Casel, who also influenced Anscar Vonier. Casel argued that the Mass is not merely the objective memorial of the Cross; yet nor is it the repetition of historical event *qua* historical. It is something midway between a pure representation of a past event and the repetition of that past event; it is, namely, the "spiritual, mystical, sacramental, metahistorical" presence of that very event.

The great difficulty with this account is to see what it could actually mean. Pius XII seems to have experienced this difficulty in *Mediator Dei*, when he criticizes certain modern authors who employ "a vague and uncertain way of speaking" about the presence of Christ's mysteries in the liturgy.[10] Also, if the Mass were numerically the same event as the Cross, would it still be essentially a pure and unbloody immolation? Maritain, presumably influenced by Casel, once went so far as to write that Christ really dies before our eyes every morning. But the Council of Trent teaches that although the victim and priest are the same now as then, the sacrifices differ in the manner of the offering, as bloody and unbloody.

The second tendency among theologians is to argue that while there is indeed a new offering at every Mass, there is, properly speaking, not a new sacrifice. An

---

[10] *AAS* 39:580. The Pope used the term "effutire," which Lewis & Short define as "to blab out, babble forth, to prate, chatter, utter."

influential twentieth-century theologian who wrote in the vein was Maurice de la Taille. He held that Christ's sacrifice consisted of two essential elements: His offering of Himself at the Last Supper, and His freely-accepted death on the Cross. As a result of the latter, Christ always remains in the state of an accepted sacrificial victim. According to de la Taille, the sacrifice of Mass arises at each new offering of this Victim by the Church.

This account is reminiscent of that of Condren, already mentioned. It differs from it, however, in that it that it considers the Church's act of consecration of the bread and wine not simply as a precondition of Christ's self-offering presence, but as itself an act of offering, which, joined to the presence of Christ who died on the Cross, forms a sacrifice, just as the offering at the Last Supper, joined to the presence of Christ who would die on the Cross, formed the same sacrifice. An objection to this view is that it makes of the Mass a renewal of the Last Supper, rather than of the Cross.

The third group of theologians hold that we must speak of a distinct sacrifice at the Mass, as well as a distinct offering or oblation. They have in their favor the language of Pius XII in *Mediator Dei*, an encyclical written after a period of intense theological discussion of this subject, who wrote: "It [the Mass] is truly and properly a sacrificing [*sacrificatio*]. The High Priest does by an unbloody immolation (*per incruentam immolationem*) that which He has already done on the Cross."[11] The pope could hardly have expressed more strongly the idea that the Mass has its own distinctive sacrificial character.

But if Holy Mass is in the proper sense a new sacrifice, this mean that not only is Christ offered, but that in some sense something is newly done to Him. For this, as St. Thomas says, is what distinguishes a sacrifice and an offering: a sacrifice is an offering which consists in something happening to what is offered. Yet of course Christ is not

---

[11] *AAS* 39:548.

changed in Himself by the fact of existing under the sacramental appearances. So how can we venture to speak of
Him being in the proper sense of the word, "sacrificed"?

Again, various theories are proposed, some of which
find little support today. One is that "what happens to
Christ" is that He is constituted as our food. Bellarmine
argued along these lines. The objection to this is that
insofar as Christ is constituted as our spiritual food, He
is not thereby offered to God, but to us; and a sacrifice
is a species of offering made to God.

Another suggestion was that our Lord is changed in
that He is put into an "inferior state" by the consecration! He is put, that is, into a state such that He can't
exercise His bodily life connaturally, since He cannot
move on the altar or speak from it without a further
miracle. This theory, which is sometimes referred to as
"moral destruction," was propounded by the Jesuit author
Francisco de Lugo. The best that can be said for it is that
it is ingenious. It has been ignored by the magisterium.

Another explanation is that what is done in regard to
Him is simply His coming to exist on the altar. One could
argue, that is, that by a positive decree of the divine will
the sacrifice of the New Covenant, that Christ comes to
be present in some place on earth by the words of consecration; that we need look no further for any explanation
of how He is said to be sacrificed. However, here again
the objection arises that the simple fact of His coming to
be present somewhere does not seem to be an offering
to God; and sacrifice is a species of offering.

At this point it is useful to recall two magisterial texts
already mentioned. The first is that of Pius XII in *Mediator
Dei*, stating that it is in virtue of the twofold consecration,
and the separated species, that the Mass represents the
Cross. The second is that of St. John Paul II in *Ecclesia de
Eucharistia*, that the Mass is itself a proper sacrifice insofar
as it is related to the Cross. Given that representation is a
kind of relation, we may deduce from this that the Mass

itself is a proper sacrifice insofar as it represents the Cross by virtue of the twofold consecration. In other words, "that which happens to Christ" is that He is *put into the state of representing His Passion*; and, of course, primarily puts Himself into this state, since He is the principal priest.

This enables us to see the depth of St. Thomas's teaching that the Mass is a sacrifice insofar as it represents the Passion. It is not that it is a mere representation, like a painting or a sculpture, but that precisely insofar as it is a representation it is also a true sacrifice, since "coming to exist in the state of representing His Passion," in virtue of the double transubstantiation, is precisely what "happens" to our Lord. Hence, the questions: "How does the Mass represent the sacrifice of the Cross?," and: "How is the Mass itself a true and proper sacrifice?" turn out to have the same answer, even though they are formally distinct questions.

Moreover, it is evident that this "being put into the state of representing the Passion" fulfils the definition of a sacrifice, since this is not simply something that happens to Christ, but rather something that happens to Him and by which very thing He is offered to God. For that was the defining feature of a sacrifice, that it is an offering of something to God, in such a way that something's being done to the thing offered actually constitutes the offering, as when an animal is said to be offered to God by the very fact of having its blood poured out upon an altar. So it is not the case that Christ simply puts Himself into the state of representing His Passion, as it were for our instruction, since that would not be an offering and therefore neither would it be a sacrifice, but that Christ puts Himself into the state of representing His Passion as the means by which He offers Himself to God. The consecration is His chosen means of offering Himself to God, and because it represents the passion and therefore is something "done in regard to" Christ, it effects a true sacrifice.

We can clarify the question by asking: "Would the Mass still be a sacrifice if the Passion had never occurred, or had never been going to occur?" The answer seems to be that if Christ had so willed, He could have made the Mass into His chosen means of offering Himself to the Father even independently of the Passion, and that this offering would still have fulfilled the criteria of a sacrifice. However, in the actual order of providence, Christ has willed that the only liturgical rite of the New Covenant by which He offers Himself should be the sacramental representation of His Passion. Therefore, we can say that in this order of providence, the Mass is not a sacrifice independently of the Cross because Christ has chosen it as His offering precisely insofar as it represents the Cross.

Finally, we can note here the relevance of what was said at the end of the previous section, that the representation of the Passion occurs not simply by virtue of the separate Eucharistic species, but by the sacramental separation of the body and blood. It is essential to a sacrifice that something is done in regard to that which is offered to God. But what is offered to God at Holy Mass is not the Eucharistic species, but the body and blood of Christ. But we have said that "what is done" at Mass is, precisely, the representation of the Passion. Therefore, it seems necessary that the representation of the Passion be made by means of our Lord's body and blood, and not simply by means of the species. Therefore, since the sacramental separation pertains to Christ Himself, since His body is the terminus of the first consecration and His blood is the terminus of the second, it is this which makes the Mass both the perfect representation of the Passion, and also, by that very fact, in the way discussed in this section, also itself a true and proper sacrifice. I end with some words of St. Gregory Nazianzen, from his 171st letter, which he wrote to a priest named Amphilochius around the year 383: "Do not fail to pray and perform your duty for us, when you draw down the Word by means of a word, and when with unbloody cutting you cut the Lord's body and blood, using of your voice as a sword."

4

The Symbolism of the First Entrance of the Holy Synaxis in the Mystagogy of St. Maximus the Confessor

REV. YOSYP VERESH

THE BYZANTINE LITURGICAL TRADITION is characterized by rich symbolism and the solemnity of various processions and entrances. In seventh-century Constantinople the Divine Liturgy began with a solemn entrance into the church.[1] This entrance was the first entrance of the patriarch with the entire congregation into the church of *Hagia Sophia*. The procession of the hierarchy and faithful, including the emperor, would assemble in the narthex; the patriarch, standing before the Royal Doors of the church would say the Introit Prayer and then he would enter the church, passing through the sanctuary and ascending to the throne.[2] At the present time, this entrance is a part of the Liturgy of the Catechumens that takes place inside the church building and is called the "small entrance." It is a procession

---

[1] See Hugh Wybrew, *The Orthodox Liturgy* (St. Vladimir's Seminary Press, 1996), 76–77.
[2] See Robert Taft, *The Byzantine Rite: A Short History* (The Liturgical Press, 1992), 34–38.

with the Gospel book from the sanctuary to the nave and then to the Royal Doors of the *iconostasys*.[3] After a prayer of entrance and blessing,[4] the procession solemnly reenters the sanctuary.

St. Maximus the Confessor—a holy monk and a distinguished theologian of the seventh century[5]—is the first to provide a full-scale interpretation of the Divine Liturgy in Constantinople in the first half of the seventh century.[6] He considers the symbolism of the "first entrance" in his work *The Church's Mystagogy* (628–630),[7] which can be divided into three parts: the first part considers the *eikons* or images of the holy Church of God (ch. 1–7); the second part gives a commentary on the Divine Liturgy (ch. 8–21); and the third part shows "how the divine precepts of the holy Church lead the soul, by a true and active knowledge, to its own perfection" (ch. 22–24).[8] It has to be mentioned that in his commentary on the Divine Liturgy St. Maximus skips the Holy Anaphora. This may be due to the fact that he is not a priest but a lay monk. Thus, he comments on those parts of the Liturgy that were open to the congregation and

---

[3] The *iconostasys* is an icon screen that separates the sanctuary from the nave of the church.

[4] The prayer and the blessing of small entrance: "O Lord, our Master and God, Who in heaven established orders and armies of angels and archangels for the service of Your glory, make this our entrance to be an entrance of holy angels, serving together with us, and with us glorifying Your goodness. For to You is due all glory, honor and worship, Father, Son and Holy Spirit, now and ever, and forever... Blessed is the entrance of Your saints, always, now and ever, and forever..." St. John Chrysostom, *The Divine Liturgy of our Father Saint John Chrysostom* (Byzantine Seminary Press, 1965), 20.

[5] See St. Maximus the Confessor, *Selected Writings* (Paulist Press, 1985), 1–11; *The Philokalia, The Complete Text*, Volume II (Faber and Faber, 1984), 48–51; Robert F. Taft, *The Byzantine Rite: A Short History*, 37.

[6] See Wybrew, *The Orthodox Liturgy*, 90.

[7] See Maximus, *The Church's Mystagogy*, in *Selected Writings*, 181–214; Wybrew, *The Orthodox Liturgy*, 95.

[8] Maximus, *The Church's Mystagogy*, ch. 22, in *Selected Writings*, 204.

the words of the Holy Anaphora were already covered by a low intonation in his time.[9]

Commenting on each part of the Divine Liturgy, St. Maximus gives two explanations: one on the "general" meaning and one on the "particular" meaning.[10] The "general" meaning refers to the mystery of salvation and the "particular" meaning refers to each individual.[11] The "general" meaning of the "first entrance" refers symbolically to the Mystery of the Incarnation. The entrance of the patriarch or the bishop into the church for the Divine Liturgy "is a figure and image of the first appearance in the flesh of Jesus Christ the Son of God and our Savior in this world."[12] It represents the Mystery of Redemption, since by his Incarnation Christ "freed human nature which had been enslaved by corruption... He redeemed all its debt as if he were liable even though He was not liable but sinless, and brought us back again to the original grace of his kingdom by giving himself as a ransom for us." It expresses the beautiful "exchange" that took place, since Christ, "in exchange for our destructive passions ... gave us His life-giving Passion as a salutary cure which saves the whole world." And finally this entrance represents the ascension of Christ "into heaven and return to the heavenly throne" which are "symbolically figured in the bishop's entrance into the sanctuary and ascent to the priestly throne."

The "particular" meaning of the "first entrance," which is the entrance of the people into the church with the bishop, symbolically represents "the conversion of the unfaithful from faithlessness to faith and from sin and error to the recognition of God as well as the passage

---

[9] See Lars Thunberg, *Man and the Cosmos: The Vision of St. Maximus the Confessor* (St. Vladimir's Seminary Press, 1985), 114.

[10] See Paul Mayendorf, *St. Germanus of Constantinople on the Divine Liturgy* (St. Vladimir's Seminary Press, 1984), 36.

[11] Ibid.

[12] Maximus, *The Church's Mystagogy*, ch. 8, in *Selected Writings*, 198; also for the following two quotations.

of the faithful from vice and ignorance to virtue and knowledge."[13] We can see in this interpretation a twofold significance: first, it signifies "the conversion of infidels to the true and only God"; and secondly, it also signifies "the amendment of each one of us who believe but who yet violate the Lord's commandments under the influence of a loose and indecent life." The second significance represents an *eikon* of Christian *metanoia*—a conversion and change of mind and life. St. Maximus writes: "...when someone is entangled in any kind of vice but should cease voluntarily to be held by its attention and deliberately to act according to it and changes his life for better by preferring virtue to vice, such a person can be properly and truly considered and spoken of as entering with Christ our God and High Priest into virtue, which is the church understood figuratively."

Our Christian journey—our spiritual entrance into the Church—begins with our Baptism into the Church when we are reborn in the Holy Spirit. St. Maximus explains in the first chapter of his *Mystagogy*: "All are born into the Church and through it are reborn and recreated in the Spirit... To all in equal measure it gives and bestows one divine form and designation, to be Christ's and to carry his name..."[14] In this the Church bears "the imprint and image of God since it has the same activity as he does by imitation and in figure."

The construction of the church building symbolically represents "the entire world composed of visible and invisible essences because like it, it contains both unity and diversity."[15] The church building symbolically represents heaven and earth: "...it has for its sanctuary the higher world assigned to the powers above, and for its nave the lower world which is reserved to those who share the life of sense."

---

[13] Ibid., 198–99, and for the next three quotations.
[14] Ibid., ch. 1, 186–87, and for the next quotation.
[15] Ibid., ch. 2, 188, and for the next quotation.

Man himself entering into the church building is a "mystical church."[16] St. Maximus compares the construction of the church to a human person: "Holy Church is like a man because for the soul it has the sanctuary, for mind (*nous*) it has the divine altar, and for body it has the nave. It is thus the image and likeness of man who is created in the image and likeness of God..."[17] In the theology of St. Maximus this threefold aspect of a church building, corresponding to the threefold aspect of a human person, corresponds also to a threefold division of Christian perfection into moral wisdom, natural contemplation and mystical theology: "By means of the nave, representing the body, it [the church] proposes moral wisdom, while by means of the sanctuary, representing the soul, it spiritually interprets natural contemplation, and by means of the mind of the divine altar it manifests mystical theology. Conversely, man is a mystical church..."[18]

The "first entrance" into the church expresses in a liturgical and symbolic way the "general" and the "particular" levels of Christian Deification. It is an expression of our recreation and rebirth into the Church by the Holy Spirit. It symbolically represents the process of our purification and illumination on the way towards an ever more perfect union with God. In this mystical assent the soul is led by Christ our High Priest, which is symbolically figured in the entrance of the people into the church together with the bishop. The "first entrance" is a liturgical expression of our spiritual progress, of our mystical entrance into the realities of supernatural and heavenly life, of our movement towards an ever intimate communion with Christ and, through Him, with the Holy Trinity. And it is possible because of the philanthropy of God revealed in the Mystery of the Incarnation and Redemption, which

---

16 Ibid., ch. 4, 190.
17 Ibid., ch. 4, 189–90.
18 Ibid., ch. 4, 190.

is also symbolically represented in the "first entrance." In the last chapter of his *Mystagogy*, St. Maximus concludes: "The first entrance of the holy synaxis which is celebrated in the church signifies in general the first appearance of Christ our God, and in particular the conversion of those who are being led by him and with him from unbelief to faith and from vice to virtue and also from ignorance to knowledge."[19]

---

[19] Ibid., ch. 24, 207.

5

Biblical and Liturgical Typology in the Letter to the Hebrews

REV. CASSIAN FOLSOM, O.S.B.

I WOULD LIKE TO TALK ABOUT BIBLICAL and liturgical typology. What that means is: How the New Testament interprets the Old and how sacraments work, with particular reference to the Eucharist. And I want to do that by looking at three chapters of the Letter to the Hebrews: chapters 8–10. These chapters are describing the superiority of Christ's sacrifice, offered in the heavenly sanctuary, superior to the many animal sacrifices offered on earth by the Levitical priests. That is the basic argument of this section, which you are more familiar with than I, because you are studying it in depth these days. This argument is rather tightly formulated, and what I would like to do is unpack it a little bit with two points of reference: one is how the Old Testament finds its fulfillment in the New and the other is how the liturgy actualizes what Christ did for us.

The chart to which I will be referring (see pp. 62–63) has three columns: Old Testament, New Testament, and Liturgy. And if you think of two arrows, the Old Testament is pointing to the New and the Liturgy is pointing to the New. Christ is at the center and we are dealing with how the Old Testament is related to the New and how the Liturgy is related to the action of Christ.

Now I will not read everything from these three chapters, but selected verses. According to the medieval

	OLD TESTAMENT	NEW TESTAMENT	LITURGY
WHO	High priest (8:1; 9:25) — *pontifex* minister (8:2) — *minister*	Christ the High Priest (9:11)	Ordained priest
WHAT		Mediator of new covenant (9:15)	
	old ministry (8:6)	more excellent ministry (8:6) — *melius ministerium*	
	old covenant (8:6) — *veterum testamentum*	new covenant (8:6) — *novum testamentum*	new and everlasting covenant — *novi et aeterni testamenti*
		better covenant (8:6) — *melius testamentu*	
	first covenant (9:1; 9:18-22) obsolete covenant (8:13), growing old — *veterum, antiquatum, senescens*		
	offers gifts & sacrifices (8:3; 8:4; 9:7; 9:9) — *ad offerendum munera et hostias*	offers himself (9:14)	offers Eucharistic sacrifice
		offering of the body of Jesus Christ (10:10)	
	blood of goats and calves (9:12)	his own blood (9:12) blood of Christ (9:14)	Eucharistic blood — *hunc calicem*
	shedding of blood (9:22)		
WHERE	sanctuary (8:2) tent (8:2; 8:5; 9:2) — *tabernaculum*	sanctuary (8:2) the true tent / his flesh greater and more perfect tent (9:11) — *tabernaculum verum*	Eucharistic body of Christ
	Outer tent (9:8) +symbolic (9:9) — *parabola est*		present age (9:8)
	second curtain / inner veil (9:3) Holy of Holies (9:3) — *sancta sanctorum*		

WHEN	repeatedly (9:25; 10:11) — *saepe* daily (10:11) — *quotidie* yearly (9:25) — *per singulos annos* continually (10:1) — *indesinenter*	once for all (9:26; 9:28; 10:10) — *semel*	as often as you shall do this — *quotiescumque feceritis* today — *hodie*
WHY	to purify from sin (cf. 9:7) purity from errors (9:7) purification of the flesh (9:13)	to put away sin once for all (9:26) to bear the sins of many (9:28)	for the forgiveness of sins — *in remissionem peccatorum* effects of the Eucharist: forgiveness of venial sin; unity of mystical Body; conformity to Christ purify conscience (9:14)
HOW	copy / copies / pattern (8:5; 9:23) — *exemplar / exemplaria* copy (9:24) — *exemplaria* shadow (8:5; 10:1) — *umbra*	heavenly things (9:23) — *caelestia* heaven itself (9:24) — *ipsum caelum* true sanctuary (9:24) — *vera sanctuaria* reality (10:1) — *res*	true form (10:1) — *ipsa imago*

ILLUSTRATIONS OF "QUOTES"

Simili modo postquam coenatum est, accipiens et *hunc praeclarum Calicem* in sanctas ac venerabiles manus suas: item tibi gratias agens, benedixit, deditque discipulis suis, dicens: Accipite et bibite ex eo omnes. Hic est enim Calix Sanguinis mei, novi et aeterni testamenti: mysterium fidei: qui pro vobis et pro multis effundetur in remissionem peccatorum. Haec *quotiescumque feceritis* in mei memoriam facietis.[1]

Concede nobis, quaesumus, Domine haec digne frequentare mysteria: quia *quoties* huius hostiae commemoratio celebratur, opus nostrae redemptionis exercetur. Per Dominum. . .[2]

SYNTHESIS: copy, shadow ——— *Holy Spirit* ——→ reality, truth ——— *Holy Spirit* ——→ sacramentum, mysterium, icon, image

[1] From the Roman Canon.   [2] *Usus antiquior:* Secreta of *Dominica IX post pentecosten; Usus recentior: In cena Domini / Dominica II per annum.*

method, a *lectio* is where you read something. So I will read something and comment on it. So my method is simple. Well, that is the simple part. There is a part that is less simple and it is somewhat artificial. That is, I have organized this handout and these categories into the questions of "who," "what," "where," "when," "why," and "how." That is the artificial part, but it might help us to see how the whole thing works.

THE LETTER TO THE HEBREWS: CHAPTER 8

HEB 8:1. "*Now the point in what we are saying is this: we have such a high priest…*" So if you consider the 'who' question, the 'who' is the high priest. And when it is useful I give the Latin and the Greek also. Sometimes it is helpful; sometimes it does not matter. So the high priest is the *pontifex*, the ἀρχιερεύς. And the Letter to the Hebrews is not so much concerned about the former high priest as about Christ the high priest, "*one who is seated at the right hand of the throne of the Majesty in heaven…*"

HEB 8:2. What is he? He is "*a minister in the sanctuary…*" So that is the second word under 'who,' "the minister." It is the same word in Latin: *minister*. In Greek it is λειτουργός, which is interesting. We have a great "liturgist" who is "*a minister in the sanctuary and the true tent…*" Now the "true tent," that has to do with 'where,' where this activity is taking place. In the Old Testament there was "the sanctuary," "the tent," "the tabernacle" of the Old Testament, which is not the true tent; it is a prefigurement. The true tent is the Lord. And, as we will see later on, the true tent is his flesh.

HEB 8:3. "*For every high priest is appointed to offer gifts and sacrifices…*" That is the question 'what,' what does he do? In the Old Testament, you see what the high priest does: he offers gifts and sacrifices. That is repeated several times in this argument. Gifts are δωρα, sacrifices θυσια. And we will see later that what Christ offers is not these gifts and sacrifices but himself. "*For every high priest is appointed to offer gifts and sacrifices; hence it is necessary for this priest also* (this priest being Christ) *to have something to offer.*"

HEB 8:4–5. "*Now if he were on earth, he would not be a priest at all, since there are priests who offer gifts according to the law.*" But "*They serve a copy and shadow of the heavenly sanctuary...*" This is technical vocabulary that is important. How does the Old Testament relate to the New? The Old Testament is a "copy" and a "shadow." Now the word "copy" in this verse is *examplar* in Latin but ὑπόδειγμα in Greek. We will see the same word used later on with a different Greek reference. So the translations do not always help; sometimes they hide the real meaning. Anyway, we have "*a copy and a shadow* (umbra) *of the heavenly sanctuary...*" So there is a copy and there is a true sanctuary. And there is the shadow and there is the reality, as we will see in chapter 10. That is really important to understand how the Old Testament relates to the New and how the liturgy relates to the action of Christ. We have a copy and a shadow which points to the truth and the reality. The liturgy, we will see, is an icon of the action of Christ. But we will get to that. "*They serve a copy and shadow of the heavenly sanctuary; for when Moses was about to erect the tent, he was instructed by God, saying, 'See that you make everything according to the pattern...'*" Now the word "pattern" is the same word as "copy"; that is, the Latin is the same: *exemplaria*; and the Greek word is the same: ὑπόδειγμα. So in English those two words are different, but in Greek they are the same. "*See that you make everything according to the pattern* (or the 'copy') *which was shown you on the mountain.*"

HEB 8:6. Now the Letter to the Hebrews is going to say that all of that is superseded. "*But as it is, Christ has obtained a ministry* (a λειτουργια) *which is as much more excellent than the old as the covenant he mediates is better...*" For there is an old ministry—an old liturgy—and there is a more excellent ministry, *melius ministerium*. There is an old covenant, *veterum testamentum*; there is a better covenant, *melius testamentum*. Now, we will see, of course, in the liturgy, the consecration of the chalice talks about the new and everlasting covenant; but we will get to that.

HEB 8:7, 13. "*For if that first covenant had been faultless, there would have been no occasion for a second.*" Let me jump to the last verse of chapter 8: "*In speaking of a new covenant he treats the first as obsolete.*" The first covenant is superseded by a better one. The first covenant then is obsolete, growing old (*veterum, antiquatum, senescens*). "*And what is becoming obsolete and growing old is ready to vanish away.*"

So far we have a partial schema of how the Old Testament relates to the New: as a foreshadowing, as a copy, as a figure of the better, more excellent, true reality which is to come.

THE LETTER TO THE HEBREWS: CHAPTER 9

HEB 9:1–5. "*Now even the first covenant* (the Old Testament) *had regulations for worship and an earthly sanctuary.*" Then it describes all the aspects of the Temple: the tent, the outer curtain; and all that is in it: the lampstand, the table, the bread of the presence, and so on. Behind the second curtain stood a tent called the holy of holies. Now I have not indicated all these different elements of the Temple because it does not pertain immediately to our argument. But all the things that were in the holy of holies were accessible only to the high priest.

HEB 9:6–7. "*These preparations having thus been made, the priests go continually into the outer tent* (that is, the ordinary priests), *performing their ritual duties; but into the second tent* (or 'veil') . . . " Under 'where,' in the Old Testament, there is the outer tent described, the sanctuary; and the second curtain, the inner veil, the holy of holies. So now "*only the high priest goes, and he but once a year, and not without taking blood which he offers for himself and for the errors of the people.*" Under the category 'why,' why does the high priest do all this? To purify from sin, to purify from errors.

HEB 9:8. And then comes a verse which is very important, which explains the interpretive key: "*By this. . .*" (that is, by the action of the high priest who offers once a year) *"the Holy Spirit indicates..."* Now that phrase is important. It is the Holy Spirit which enables the passage from the Old Testament to the New, from type to reality. It is the same Holy Spirit which enables the action of the liturgy to have its efficacy. The liturgy is an icon or image of the action of Christ, which we have access to by the power of the Holy Spirit. So that is an interpretive key here. *"By this the Holy Spirit indicates that the way into the sanctuary is not yet opened as long as the outer tent is still standing (which is symbolic for the present age)."* The word "symbolic" is under 'where,' the outer tent. And the tent is "symbolic" (in Latin: *parabola est*; and the word is the same in Greek: παραβολη). So the Letter is using this symbolic language very deliberately to make a distinction between the Old Testament and the New. So this outer tent and all that goes on with the high priest entering into the inner tent is symbolic, is a parable, of the reality.

HEB 9:9–11. *"According to this arrangement, gifts and sacrifices are offered which cannot perfect the conscience of the worshipper* (the implication is that Christ's sacrifice can), *but deal only with food and drink and various ablutions..."* and so on. *"But when Christ appeared as a high priest of the good things that have come..."* In the New Testament you have Christ the high priest. You see in the Old Testament there was a high priest; now you have Christ the high priest. *"He enters through the greater and more perfect tent..."* Under 'where,' it is no longer the sanctuary of the Old Testament, called a "tent"; but the "true tent," a greater and more perfect tent, the *tabernaculum verum*. And the Greek adjective for true is ἀληθινη.

HEB 9:12. Christ entering through this tent *"entered once for all into the holy place..."* Now that "once for all" is very important too. We will see in this discourse on chapters 9 and 10 a contrast asserted over and over again between sacrifices that were offered repeatedly, daily, yearly, continually; and the sacrifice offered *semel*, ἀπαξ, once and for all. Now if you are thinking ahead, you would think of the Eucharist that is offered every day, or at least frequently, and you would ask yourself: How does that fit into the ἅπαξ? Is that the same as all these other things that repeat continually, that we are saying are superseded? That is an important question because that refers to how the liturgy works. But we will get there. So he offers once for all, *semel*. *"Taking not the blood of goats and calves but his own blood..."* What is offered? It is the body of Jesus Christ that is offered, as we will see in chapter 10; that is, his own blood. Taking *"his own blood, thus securing an eternal redemption."*

HEB 9:13–14. *"For if the sprinkling of defiled persons with the blood of goats and bulls and with the ashes of a heifer sanctifies for the purification of the flesh..."* That was the purpose of all of this in the Old Testament, the purification of the flesh. *"How much more* (contrast) *shall the blood of Christ purify, who through the eternal Spirit offered himself without blemish to God."* So what will Christ accomplish? He will *"purify your conscience from dead works to serve the living God."* If you look at the 'why' of all of this, in the Old Testament you have purification of the flesh; but Christ purifies from sin, once for all. He purifies our conscience. He bears the sins of many.

HEB 9:15–17. *"Therefore he is the mediator of a new covenant..."* So Christ the high priest is also the mediator of a new covenant, *"so that those who are called may receive the promised eternal inheritance..."* Then he goes into the argument about the nature of a will, and so on.

HEB 9:18–20. *"Hence even the first covenant was not ratified without blood..."* And Moses said to the people: *"This is the blood of the covenant which God commanded you."* So there is the blood of the old covenant which does not have the power to purify; and there is the blood of the new covenant which is the blood of Christ and, as we will see, is also the eucharistic blood.

HEB 9:21–22. *"In the same way Moses sprinkled with the blood both the tent and all the vessels used in worship. Indeed, under the law almost everything is purified with blood, and without the shedding of blood there is no forgiveness of sins."* So that is the purpose of these sacrifices also: the purpose in the Old Testament, which the Letter to the Hebrews is arguing is ineffective; and the blood of Christ which was effective *semel,* once and for all, which (we will get to it) the liturgy participates in.

HEB 9:23. *"Thus it was necessary for the copies of the heavenly things..."* We are back to "copies" now. How does all of this work? By copies indicating the reality. *"It was necessary for the copies of these things to be purified with these rites, but the heavenly things themselves..."* This is τα πραγματα, the reality. Now the Latin word for reality is *res,* but it is not the same—be careful, you scholars of St. Thomas—it is not the same as the sacramental category of *res* in scholastic sacramental theology. Even though it is the same word, it does not mean the same thing, so be careful. In this case it means the reality of Christ's action.

HEB 9:24. *"For Christ has entered, not into a sanctuary made with hands, a copy of the true one..."* (so there is the 'copy' and the 'true'), *but into heaven itself, now to appear in the presence of God on our behalf."* It is clear that the sacrifice of Christ on the cross and his death and resurrection and his ascension into heaven are all part of the same action.

HEB 9:25–26. *"Nor was it to offer himself repeatedly"* (saepe), *as the high priest did... for then he would have had to suffer repeatedly* (saepe, πολλακις in Greek) *since the foundation of the world. But as it is, he has appeared once for all* (semel, ἀπαξ) *at the end of the age to put away sin by the sacrifice of himself."* So his own body and his own blood is the sacrifice, and the purpose of that is to put away sin. Under the 'why' category, it was to put away sin once for all, to bear the sins of many, as we will see; that is the purpose of Christ's action.

HEB 9:27–28. *"And just as it is appointed for men to die once, and after that comes judgment, so Christ having been offered once* (semel) *to bear the sins of many* (that is the purpose of his action) *will appear a second time..."* for judgment.

THE LETTER TO THE HEBREWS: CHAPTER 10

HEB 10:1. "*Since the law has but a shadow* (umbra) *of the good things to come* (τα πραγματα) . . . *"* There is the contrast between the shadow, which points to the reality; that is, these actions of Christ. And I will get to the liturgical part in just a moment. Now let us look at that one verse again; there is a lot in it: "*Since the law has but a shadow of the good things to come* (that is, the reality) . . . *"* Where, as we will see, the liturgy is the form of these realities. Now perhaps I am doing violence to the text for the sake of liturgical theology, but the fathers certainly use this kind of language to describe how *sacramentum* or *mysterium*, how the sacraments work as an icon of the reality. Just as Christ is the icon of the Father, so also the sacraments work as an icon, an image, a true form, of the action of Christ and participate in it by the power of the Holy Spirit, as we will see. Once again: "*Since the law has but a shadow of the good things to come instead of the true form of these realities, it can never, by the same sacrifices which are continually offered year after year* (repeatedly, daily, yearly, continually) *make perfect those who draw near."*

HEB 10:9-10. After the citation of the Psalm, "*Lo I have come to do Thy will,*" it says, "*He abolishes the first* (sacrifice) *in order to establish the second. And by that will we have been sanctified through the offering of the body of Jesus Christ* (that is what is offered now, not the blood of goats and calves, but the body of Christ) *once and for all* (semel)."

HEB 10:11-14. "*Every priest stands daily at his service* (Old Testament priests), *offering repeatedly the same sacrifices* (it is the same vocabulary again: repeatedly, daily, yearly, continually, *indesinentes*), *which can never take away sins. But when Christ had offered for all time a single sacrifice for sins, he sat down at the right hand of God... For by a single offering he has perfected for all time those who are sanctified."*

That is all of the text that I am going to read. Now what we have done so far is to try to establish how the New Testament interprets the Old. In this particular case, how the high priest is related to Christ the high priest; how the old ministry, the old liturgy, points to the new ministry, the more excellent liturgy; how the first covenant is superseded by the better covenant; how instead of offering the blood of goats and calves, Christ offers himself, his own body and his own blood; how the former tent is superseded by the true tent which is the flesh of Christ. St. John's Gospel (the language of which is not referred to here) makes a very clear point that the Temple is superseded by the body of Christ, which is the true Temple. The word "temple" is not used in these chapters here, but it is the same argument. All of these Old Testament things are symbolic, are parables, are shadows, are images that point to the reality. And the reality happens once for all.

THE LITURGY AS AN ICON OF THE ACTION OF CHRIST

Now let us go to the liturgical aspect of things, which is not immediately obvious perhaps just from reading the text itself. Now ask yourselves a question as we go through this. I am going to affirm that certain things happen, but the question is: How does it happen? And hopefully we will get to the 'how' question at the end. For the time being I am just going to affirm that it happens.

WHO. So the ordained priest in the liturgy participates in the priesthood of Christ, Christ the high priest. In the Mass the new and everlasting covenant celebrated in the Eucharist is offered to us. We participate in the new covenant of the death and resurrection of Christ. On your handout you have the words of consecration from the Roman canon over the chalice because you have the words "the blood of the new and everlasting covenant." Look at the middle of the consecratory prayer: *Hic est enim Calix Sanguinis mei, novi et aeterni testamenti* (the chalice of my blood, the chalice of the new and everlasting covenant). So that lines up perfectly with the old covenant that is superseded by the new, the action of Christ; and in the Eucharist this new covenant, then, is offered to us, is presented to us for us to participate in.

WHAT. In the Eucharist the priest offers the eucharistic sacrifice; in the Old Testament the priest offers these gifts and sacrifices; in the New Testament Christ offers himself. In the Mass the priest offers the eucharistic sacrifice (we offer ourselves too, but that will become more clear I hope when we ask the question 'how'). In the Eucharist we offer the eucharistic body and blood of Christ; and there is a clue in the precise language of the consecration of the chalice: *Simili modo postquam coenatum est, accipiens hunc praeclarum Calicem* ("this one"). Now that is very strange, because obviously, when the priest uses a chalice in the Eucharist, it is not the same chalice that Christ used at the Last Supper. But the liturgy affirms that it is, *hunc*, this one right here, because the liturgy is bridging the time gap between today and the action of Christ, affirming that it is the same. The 'how' question comes at the end, remember, but this is an affirmation that what we do in the Mass is participating in the action of Christ and it is the same: *hunc*, this chalice. That is important.

WHEN. Then we have the whole question of time, the 'when' question, because the Old Testament sacrifices are offered repeatedly, daily, yearly, continually; but Christ's sacrifice is *semel*, ἅπαξ, unique, once for all. Then why does the liturgy use language of repetition and say, as often as you shall do this (*quotiescumque*). After the consecration of the chalice, there is this citation from the Gospel that says, *Haec quotiescumque feceritis*, as often as you do these things; not just once, not *semel*, not ἅπαξ, but often; as often as you do this, you will do it (*facietis*) *in mei memoriam*. So we have to reconcile repetition, frequency, often, with the ἅπαξ somehow. How do we do that? Well, one of the ways that the liturgy does that is with the word *hodie*, or today. In the Old Testament you have sacrifices offered daily; Christ's sacrifice is just once, ἅπαξ; the liturgy affirms that what we do today is what Christ did ἅπαξ, once. And the liturgy does that, especially in the liturgy of the hours, by antiphons that celebrate *hodie*. So in the liturgical year there are lots of antiphons that begin: *Hodie*, today something happens.

And I have photocopied for you one antiphon only, from the Christmas vespers, which is repeated every day of the Christmas octave (unless the three companions of Christ intervene; that is, the Innocents, St. Stephen, and St. John; on those days you have the antiphon from the feast, but otherwise it is the *Hodie*). And when I was a young monk I thought it very strange that it was not Christmas at all and we kept saying "today . . . today . . . today." Look at the antiphon, which is very lovely: *Hodie Christus natus est.* Today Christ was born. *Hodie Salvator apparuit.* Today the Savior has appeared. *Hodie in terra canunt Angeli, laetantur Archangeli.* Today the Angels sing on the earth and the Archangels rejoice. *Hodie exsultant justi, dicentes Gloria in excelsis Deo.* Today the just rejoice, singing glory to God in the highest. If we were going to be very good Cartesian rationalists, we would say: it is not *hodie* at all. But of course the liturgy does not work that way. It insists over and over again, four times in this antiphon: "today." Time is being bridged over here. The gap is being bridged over between the liturgical mystery being celebrated today (in this case Christmas) and ἅπαξ (what happens once and for all).

Now this is not strictly speaking the Eucharist, but liturgical feasts. And St. Leo the Great will give some clues as to how that happens. When we celebrate the liturgical year (take Christmas, for example, which affirms that Christmas happens today), he says, there are two things that contribute to making this efficacious: that is, the year itself that goes on its merry way, as it turns around on its cycle it brings back the feast to us. That is why we celebrate Christmas every year, because it comes back. The earth goes around the sun and these things go in a cycle and it comes back to us. That very action of the created universe presents the feast to us again. That is one thing: it comes around. And the second thing Leo emphasizes is that the Gospel reading of the day presents these events as if they were before our very eyes. So you have two things: you have the created universe and you have a Gospel text and those two things help to bridge this gap of time and render what Christ did once and for all, *semel*, available to us today.

WHY. If we pull all of this together, the 'why' is for the forgiveness of sins, because in the prayer of consecration it says: *qui pro vobis et pro multis effundetur* (that is, the blood of Christ)... Why? *In remissionem peccatorum*. For the remission of sins. So the effects of the Eucharist, as we see in the postcommunion prayers, are the forgiveness of sin (that is, venial sin) and unity and charity; not just unity and charity among each other — that is important too — but unity with the Trinity and entering into the life of the Trinity in the Holy Spirit. So those are the effects of the Eucharist. But it happens because the Eucharist is an image, an icon, of what Christ did *semel*, once and for all.

HOW. Now how does this happen? I promised I would say something about how, and I will say something, but you could develop it at great length. In the Old Testament the copies and the shadows point to the reality and the truth of Christ by means of the Holy Spirit. That is what was affirmed in chapter 9 of the Letter to the Hebrews. In the same way in the Eucharist, or in the liturgical year, or in the sacraments, what we celebrate is a *sacramentum* or *mysterium* or icon or image; that is, some kind of material reality — sacraments are about things that you can touch. These external signs communicate the reality, make the reality available to us. And in the Eucharist the Holy Scriptures identify this eucharistic body of Christ with the earthly and resurrected body of Christ. How does it happen? Once again, by the Holy Spirit. That is not developed here in these chapters, but just hinted at. That is the task of sacramental theology to investigate more precisely how that happens.

CONCLUSION

In this little romp through three chapters of the Letter to the Hebrews, I have tried to do three things, very simple things. The first one is to see how the New Testament interprets the Old; that is, the spiritual interpretation of the Scriptures. That is very important. It is an art that has been in large part forgotten, but the fathers use it all the time; that is, they read the Old Testament through a certain lens, from the Christian point of view, from the point of view of Christ and his salvific activity for us. If you read the Old Testament that way, then it becomes alive and is not simply a somewhat curious document with all sorts of sometimes bizarre information. It is not only that. You can read it as literature and be fascinated by it because it is really splendid. But it is more than that. It is our story that Christ makes alive for us. So that is the first point; that is, the spiritual interpretation of the Scripture: how the New Testament interprets the Old. We are not making this up, the spiritual interpretation of the Scriptures. That is what the New Testament does with the Old. So if we read we discover the method that we need in order to read.

The second point is the typological understanding of the liturgy; that is, how the liturgy works. It works through typology. Baptism has all these Scriptural references to water: the Red Sea, the Flood. The New Testament points to those things and says: See, this is about baptism. Once again, that is how the New Testament reads the Old. The same thing happens in the liturgy; that is, the action of Christ, at the center of reality, at the center of time, at the center of the cosmos, which happened once and for all, has to be available to us in some way. How do we participate in that? Here is the real meaning of participation, quite different from superficial meanings that tend to be much more common; that is, the liturgy, by its typological, sacramental use of created reality, by the return of the liturgical year, by the Scriptures read to us, allows us to participate in the action of Christ by the Holy Spirit. That is true participation. And that is what we earnestly want when we go to Mass, to participate in this fundamental reality which is the action of Christ, which is — to use a phrase coined in the last fifty years; a very useful phrase if understood in the right way — the paschal mystery. That is what we are after and the liturgy allows us to enter into that. So that was the second point, how the liturgy uses typology to allow us to participate.

The third point I have already anticipated. It is the role of the Holy Spirit as an interpretive principle; that is, the Old Testament points to the New by means of the Holy Spirit enlightening us to understand. The liturgy gives us access to Christ by means of the Holy Spirit also. That whole theology of the Holy Spirit could be much more developed than it tends to be in our theological discourse. But that is the task of theologians.

6

The Christian Liturgy as *Sacrificium Laudis* in the Epistle to the Hebrews

PETER A. KWASNIEWSKI

WHERE IS THE CHRISTIAN LITURGY IN the Epistle to the Hebrews, or, to put the question more sharply, where is the Holy Sacrifice of the Mass?

We can find manifest evidence of liturgical worship and the Mass in other parts of the New Testament—one need only think of the transformation of the Passover narrated in the Synoptic Gospels; the singing of a hymn at the end of the Last Supper; the motif of "breaking bread" in Luke and the Acts of the Apostles; St. Paul's statement to the Corinthians that he is handing down to them a sacred rite that he himself received, which involves discerning the Body and Blood of the Lord in the food and drink placed before us, lest we sin against the reality present; the extravagantly liturgical symbolism of the Book of Revelation, which conveys its hidden message using signs of worship familiar to the early Christians.[1]

In contrast, the Epistle to the Hebrews places so much emphasis on explaining how the unique sacrificial death

---

[1] On this point, see Scott Hahn, *The Lamb's Supper: The Mass as Heaven on Earth* (Doubleday, 1999); Peter Kwasniewski, "Enter His Courts With Praise: Liturgical Reverence for Christ the King," *New Liturgical Movement*, May 2, 2022, https://www.newliturgicalmovement.org/2022/05/enter-his-courts-with-praise-liturgical.html.

of Christ the new and eternal High Priest released us from the vain repetition of the old covenant animal sacrifices that we might find ourselves wondering what room is left in the world for *any* kind of sacrifice, any religious cult or ritual offering or priestly office. It seems that Our Lord has simply done everything, once and for all, leaving us with the easy task of sitting back and accepting that He has done it and that we are saved by our faith in Him.

This is perhaps a tempting approach for those who have not given the matter much thought. But there are obvious problems with it. First, the fact that Our Lord has made the perfect sacrifice only means that He Himself has fulfilled all the requirements for perfectly pleasing God; it does not mean (at least it *need* not mean) that any one of us has yet benefited from his action, such as to be made pleasing to God ourselves. To benefit from an action performed by a person independently of us, this action somehow has to become *our* action; it has to be made our own in some meaningful sense, if we wish to obtain its fruits. Christ's God-pleasingness has to become our God-pleasingness.

Second, Jesus has already finished the course of His life, He has done what God sent Him into the world to accomplish, and has returned in glory to the Father (or rather, has exalted His human nature to the fullest participation of that divine glory from which, as Son, He had never departed). We who are alive right now, however, are still running our course. We have not finished the race, and we are still far from the fatherland. We ourselves *owe* something to God who made us and who calls us to redemption: we owe Him our thoughts, our volitions, our good actions, our life, our very being; we owe him our faith, our prayer, our worship—in short, the sacrifice of our own hearts. To be a Christian in deed and not in name alone, we have to do what Christ did—we must die on the Cross with him. The good news is *not* that we have nothing to do, but that Christ has already done the work perfectly and has given us a clear and attainable way to make His work our own.

If we might dare to summarize the life of the Christian, it is the putting on of Christ. It is the living of Christ's life by the gift of His grace (which, coming to us through His divinized soul, conforms us to His sonship), and the exercising of Christ's virtues, with charity and religion at the head of them.

The virtue of charity is familiar to all and frequently commented on, but nowadays one seldom hears much discussion of the virtue of religion. Yet St. Thomas Aquinas dedicates to this virtue and its attendant interior and exterior acts a surprisingly lengthy treatise in the Secunda Secundae of the *Summa theologiae*, spanning an impressive 71 articles.[2] Perhaps it is surprising only to modern Christians, who think that when we have said "faith, hope, and charity," we have covered everything there is to be covered. What we forget is that man, as a creature, as a rational animal, has innate obligations to worship God in a manner dictated by Him and pleasing to Him; that this is a form of justice, whereby we strive to give to God what is due to Him, to the best of our ability; and that we finite and fallen children of Adam are, in a way, set up for failure unless we can attach ourselves to *Christ's* exercise of the virtue of religion, which is not only perfect in every way, but overflowingly superabundant, far in excess of what any creature can give. The reason is that he is no mere creature, but a man who is God, a man whose being or *esse* is the being

---

[2] Question 81 (8 articles) deals with the virtue of religion itself; questions 82–83 deal with interior acts of religion (devotion, 4 articles; prayer, 17 [!] articles); questions 84–91 with exterior acts of religion (adoration, 3 articles; sacrifice, 4 articles; oblations and first-fruits, 4 articles; tithes, 4 articles; vows, 12 articles; oaths, 10 articles; taking God's name by adjuration, 3 articles; invoking God's name with praise, 2 articles). This is a total of 71 articles given over to the virtue of religion.

of God.[3] One might say that Jesus Christ has fulfilled, once and for all, any and every demand of the virtue of religion, such that the entire universe of intellectual creatures can feast forever off of this surplus of virtue.

The key thing is that they have to come to the feast: they have a job to do, which is to take what Christ has done and make it their own — naturally, with His help — so that, as St. Paul says, "it is no longer I who live, but Christ who lives in me" (Gal 2:20). St. Paul might just as truthfully have said: "it is not I who love, but Christ who loves in me; it is not I who worship, but Christ who worships in me." In speaking thus, Paul is not denying that we continue to live, love, and worship with our own internal principles, our own substantial being with its panoply of accidents.[4] He is emphasizing that *another* principle has been grafted onto us, inserted *within* us, at the very root of our souls where grace perfects the intellectual substance,[5] so that what we do from our own creaturely principles, we may now *also* do from, with, and towards God. The most characteristic tenet of the Catholic doctrine of grace is just this insistence, following the lead of the second epistle of St. Peter, that God really and truly imparts to man a share in His own holiness, in a way that transforms us from inside out, and makes us, not putatively or legally, but ontologically and actually, His own beloved sons, *filii in Filio*. As St. Peter says:

> May grace and peace be multiplied to you in
> the knowledge of God and of Jesus our Lord.
> His divine power has granted to us all things

---

[3] See *ST* III, q. 17; cf. J. L. A. West, "Aquinas on the Metaphysics of *Esse* in Christ," *The Thomist* 66 (2002): 231–50.

[4] See St. Thomas's commentary on Galatians 2:20.

[5] See *ST* I-II, q. 110, a. 4: "For as man in his intellective powers participates in the divine knowledge through the virtue of faith, and in his power of will participates in the divine love through the virtue of charity, so also in the nature of the soul does he participate in the divine nature, after the manner of a likeness, through a certain regeneration or re-creation."

that pertain to life and godliness, through the knowledge of him who called us to his own glory and excellence, by which he has granted to us his precious and very great promises, that through these you may escape from the corruption that is in the world because of passion, and become partakers of the divine nature. (2 Pet 1:2–4)

"Partakers of the divine nature": this means, among other things, that we are raised up to sit with Christ in the heavenly places,[6] equipped to act as the God-man acts, ready and eager to join in with the perfect worship of the heavenly Jerusalem, the perpetual intercession of the wounded Lamb, the never-ending praise of the Church Triumphant.

Where do we find these wonderful truths in the Epistle to the Hebrews itself? Put differently, *how* does Hebrews address the exercise of the virtue of religion and the specifically Eucharistic modality in which it is to be exercised? The place to look is chapter 13, which has a rich teaching on the sacrificial dimension of the Christian life and how it relates to the work of Christ the Savior. Let us go through Hebrews 13:9–16 carefully. First, I will read the whole passage (using the Douay-Rheims translation), and then I will walk through it in segments.

9 For it is best that the heart be established with grace, not with meats; which have not profited those that walk in them.

10 We have an altar, whereof they have no power to eat who serve the tabernacle.

11 For the bodies of those beasts, whose blood is brought into the holies by the high priest for sin, are burned without the camp.

12 Wherefore Jesus also, that he might sanctify the people by his own blood, suffered without the gate.

---

[6] See Eph 2:6; cf. 1:3, 1:20.

> 13 Let us go forth therefore to him without the camp, bearing his reproach.

> 14 For we have not here a lasting city, but we seek one that is to come.

> 15 By him, therefore, let us offer the sacrifice of praise always to God, that is to say, the fruit of lips confessing to his name.

> 16 And do not forget to do good, and to impart; for by such sacrifices God's favour is obtained.

Take the first four verses.

> 9 For it is best that the heart be established with grace, not with meats; which have not profited those that walk in them.

> 10 **We have an altar**, whereof they have **no power to eat** who **serve the tabernacle**.

> 11 For the <u>bodies</u> of those beasts, whose <u>blood</u> is brought into the holies by the high priest for sin, are burned without the camp.

> 12 Wherefore Jesus also, that he might sanctify the people <u>by his own blood</u>, suffered without the gate.

P. C. Yorke explains: "Priest, victim and altar go together, and therefore when St. Paul says that the early Christian had an altar, he implies that they had also a victim and a priest."[7] The text uses the present tense: we *have* an altar from which we have the power to eat (or the "right" to eat, as the RSV translates it), in contrast to those who follow the now-superseded Mosaic sacrificial law and put their trust in its animal offerings. Those who partake of the new altar are establishing their hearts in grace, not looking for help in the charred remains characteristic of the old altar. (The New International Version has a nice way of bringing out the meaning of verse 9: "It is good

---

[7] P. C. Yorke, *Altar and Priest* (The Text Book Publishing Co., 1913), 233.

for our hearts to be strengthened by grace, not by eating
ceremonial foods, which is of no benefit to those who
do so.") But so far from abolishing sacrifice, the letter
goes out of its way to state that Jesus imitates the animal
sacrifices by suffering outside the gate, as the bodies of
the animals are burned outside the camp.[8] Moreover,
even as the high priest brings the animals' blood into the
holies (or the sanctuary), with a hope of the remission of
sins, so Jesus, both high priest and victim, sanctifies the
people by His own blood, achieving the full remission of
sins. The text speaks in the subjunctive: that Jesus *might
sanctify* the people, implying that their sanctification is
still in progress: it is still to be accomplished in those
who, having access to the altar, eat of its victim.

In doing this, we share in the passion and death of
our Lord, as the text goes on to say:

> 13 Let us **go forth** [now] therefore **to him /
> without the camp** [that is, to Calvary], **bear-
> ing his reproach** [i.e., participating in His
> self-emptying].

Note the tone of urgency: there is something we ourselves
must be doing now: going out to meet Christ. Where
is He? The letter tells us that we are to seek Him in the
heavenly Jerusalem, which is described in vividly liturgical
language, reminiscent of the Apocalypse of John:

> 14 For we have not **here** a lasting **city**, but we
> seek one that is to come. [This line clearly refers
> back to what the author had said in the pre-
> ceding chapter:

> 22 But you have come to Mount Zion and to
> the city of the living God, the heavenly Jeru-
> salem, and to innumerable angels in festal
> gathering,

---

[8] It would be more accurate to say that the animal sacrifices were
set up as they were so that later, in the fullness of time, Christ
could follow them in certain respects, for our instruction.

> 23 and to the <u>assembly of the first-born</u> who are
> enrolled in heaven, and to a judge who is God of
> all, and to the spirits of just men made perfect,
>
> 24 and to Jesus, the mediator of a new covenant,
> and to the **sprinkled blood** that **speaks** more
> graciously than the blood of Abel. (12:22–24)]

Jesus is presented here as the one who *is* the mediator of a new covenant — His mediation has not ended
and will never end. The new covenant in His blood is
not a past act but a permanent state or condition of
the redeemed soul: His "sprinkled blood" (evoking the
ritual action of the old covenant, by which the people
had to be marked with the sacrificial blood in order to
benefit from the offering, as if its blood became theirs)
speaks more graciously than Abel's. It speaks right now,
and forever. Whatever this mysterious "speech" of the
Blood of Christ may be, it is an ongoing act of speaking,
one that covers us, heals us, elevates us, and divinizes
us. It is the life-giving word of the living Word, poured
out from His Heart. In the dense language of this epistle, we are being told that Christian worship is a way
of entering, even now, into the everlasting city, a festal
gathering of angels and of the congregation of firstborn
sons, so that the power of the Blood of the Lamb may
continually be communicated to us, and we in turn may
commune with it.

Next, the climactic verse 15:

> 15 **By him**, therefore, **let us offer the sacrifice
> of praise always to God,** that is to say, the fruit
> of lips confessing to his name.

As much as to say: Because all of these things are true,
let us now offer up, by (or through) Christ, the *sacrificium
laudis*, the sacrifice of praise, to God. Christ Himself is
already offering this *sacrificium laudis* and we get to participate in it. Moreover, we are to do this *always* (the RSV
has "continually"): it is an activity for the whole of our

lives, not a one-time action. Notice, too, how St. Paul glosses *sacrificium laudis* as "the fruit of lips confessing to his name." The sacrifice is not *equated* with verbal confession, but is said to be the *fruit* of a bodily action of confessing or acknowledging God's name. This could be saying to us that there must first be an interior act of faith and, second, an external expression of that faith, before it is possible to offer, in truth, a sacrifice of praise.[9] That would make the "sacrifice of praise" something more than a mere verbal offering.

Before continuing with my exegesis of Hebrews 13:15, I would like to draw attention to a number of verses from the Old Testament that use the expression *sacrificum laudis* or something quite similar. "Offer to God the sacrifice of praise: and pay thy vows to the most High" (Ps 49:14). "The sacrifice of praise shall glorify me: and there is the way by which I will show him the salvation of God" (Ps 49:23). "And let them sacrifice the sacrifice of praise: and declare his works with joy" (Ps 106:22). "I will sacrifice to thee the sacrifice of praise, and I will call upon the name of the Lord" (Ps 115:8). "And offer a sacrifice of praise with leaven: and call free offerings, and proclaim it: for so you would do, O children of Israel, saith the Lord God" (Amos 4:5). "But I with the voice of praise will sacrifice to thee: I will pay whatsoever I have vowed for my salvation to the Lord" (Jonah 2:10). "And thou hast taken pity upon two only children. Make them, O Lord, bless thee more fully: and to offer up to thee a sacrifice of thy praise, and of their health, that all nations may know, that thou alone art God in all the earth" (Tob 8:19).[10] What strikes me about such Old Testament verses is how frequently and thoroughly their language is present in the historic Christian liturgies, intimately incorporated into their fabric. Here are three

---

[9] If this is a correct reading, it would parallel Aquinas's treatment of the interior and exterior acts of religion.

[10] From this passage is derived the Introit for the Nuptial Mass.

of many examples: the short responsory at Vespers for the Common of Confessor Bishops ("R. The Lord chose him * For a priest unto Himself. The Lord chose. V. To offer unto Him the sacrifice of praise. For a priest. Glory be to the Father. The Lord chose."[11]); the Secret of the Mass *Os justi* ("In memory of Thy Saints, O Lord, we offer to Thee the sacrifice of praise, by which we trust to be freed from both present and future evils"[12]); the Offertory of the Mass for the Dead ("We offer to Thee, O Lord, sacrifices and prayers of praise: do Thou receive them on behalf of those souls of whom we make memorial this day. O Lord, make them pass over from death to life, as you promised to Abraham and his seed").[13]

It is therefore eminently reasonable to assume that Hebrews 13:15 is speaking obliquely of the offering of the Mass,[14] which from the earliest centuries was called the *sacrificium laudis*, as we see in one of the most ancient anaphoras, the Roman Canon, in the prayer known as the Commemoration of the Living:

> Memento, Domine, famulorum famularumque tuarum *N.* et *N.*, et omnium circumstantium, quorum tibi fides cognita est et nota devotio:

---

[11] ℞. *Elegit eum Dominus * Sacerdotem sibi. Elegit. ℣. Ad sacrificandum ei hostiam laudis. Sacerdotem. Gloria Patri. Elegit.*

[12] *Laudis tibi, Domine, hostias immolamus in tuorum commemoratione sanctorum: quibus nos et praesentibus exui malis confidimus et futuris.*

[13] *Hostias et preces tibi, Domine, laudis offerimus: tu suscipe pro animabus illis, quarum hodie memoriam facimus: fac eas, Domine, de morte transire ad vitam. Quam olim Abrahae promisisti et semini ejus.*

[14] As other commentators have also argued, such as Shane Kapler in *The Epistle to the Hebrews and the Seven Core Beliefs of Catholics* (Angelico Press, 2016), 101–17. Curiously, St. Thomas Aquinas in his commentary on Hebrews takes this verse and the surrounding context to refer to sanctifying grace, the Cross, or Christ Himself, but does not make much of a connection with the Eucharistic liturgy. See *Commentary on the Letter of Saint Paul to the Hebrews*, trans. F. R. Larcher, O.P., ed. J. Mortensen and E. Alarcón (Lander, WY: The Aquinas Institute for the Study of Sacred Doctrine, 2012), ch. 13, lec. 2, nos. 740–54. In no. 744, he does insinuate a liturgical connection by referencing 1 Cor 11:29.

> pro quibus tibi offerimus, vel qui tibi oferunt
> **hoc sacrificium laudis,** pro se suisque omnibus:
> pro redemptione animarum suarum, pro spe
> salutis et incolumitatis suae: tibique reddunt
> vota sua aeterno Deo, vivo et vero.

> Remember, O Lord, Thy servants and hand-
> maids, *N.* and *N.*, and all here present, whose
> faith and devotion are known to Thee; for whom
> we offer, or who offer up to Thee, **this sacrifice
> of praise** for themselves and all who are theirs,
> for the redemption of their souls, for the hope
> of their salvation and safety, and who pay their
> vows to Thee, the eternal God, living and true.[15]

We know that for a sacrament to take place, there must
be a correct intention (internal element) and the correct
matter and form (external element). Like many other
missal prayers to which one could look, the Memento
expresses this duality by mentioning "faith," which is the
root internal virtue, and "devotion" which is one of the
interior acts of religion, by which man subjects himself
wholly to God; as Aquinas puts it, devotion is "the will
to give oneself readily to things concerning the service
of God."[16] God alone sees this faith and devotion. Then
there is the external act, visible to all, consisting of the
offering of bread and wine, determined to their sacrificial
finality both by the words of consecration subsequent
to the Memento, and by the proleptic oblation of the
Offertory rite.

Nicholas Gihr provides a splendid meditation on this
prayer:

> The priest and the faithful offer to the Lord the
> sacrifice of praise now prepared on the altar
> (*hoc sacrificium laudis*). The Mass is the infinitely
> perfect sacrifice of praise and adoration, which

---

[15] Note how closely this language tracks Ps 49:14 and Jonah 2:10,
quoted above.
[16] See *ST* II-II, q. 82, a. 1.

we offer to the glory of the Most High. When
the wise man exhorts us: "Glorify the Lord as
much as ever you can, for He will yet far exceed,
and His magnificence is wonderful. Blessing the
Lord, exalt Him as much as you can; for He
is above all praise" (Ecclus. 43:32–33), we may
boldly and cheerfully answer: Here on the altar
there is offered to God a praise worthy of His
greatness, because it is infinite and divine, since
it is the sacrifice of His only-begotten Son. When
the Lord laid "the foundations of the earth . . .
the morning stars praised [Him] together, and
all the sons of God [the angels] made a joyful
melody" (Job 38:4, 7); but the chant of praise
of the heavenly hosts is not to be compared with
the adoration, homage, and glorification that
ascend from the altar to heaven. By the Eucharistic sacrifice of praise the name of the Lord is
magnified "from the rising of the sun unto the
going down of the same" (Ps 112:3).[17]

We can summarize by saying that the *sacrificium laudis*
does involve verbal praise, since a rational sacrifice always
includes the word. But in Romans 12:1, we are told that
our "rational worship" (or "reasonable service" in the
Douay Rheims) is "to present our *bodies* [as] a living sacrifice, holy, pleasing unto God," and Hebrews 12:24 tells
us that the blood of Jesus *speaks.* The offering of the body
and blood *is* the offering of the Logos.[18] Jesus became
our mediator by taking on flesh and blood; we therefore
must take on *His* flesh and blood to enter with Him into
heaven: "Having therefore, brethren, a confidence in the
entering into the holies by the *blood* of Christ—a new
and living way which he hath dedicated for us through
the veil, that is to say, his *flesh*" (Heb 10:19–20). The text

---

[17] Nicholas Gihr, *The Holy Sacrifice of the Mass, Dogmatically, Litur-
gically, and Ascetically Explained* (Herder, 1949), 644–45.
[18] Hebrews intends for us to see a marvelous parallel between
Mount Sinai and Mount Sion. On the top of Sinai speaks the
voice of God; on the top of Sion speaks the voice of the Blood.

compels us to ask, quite literally, "How *on earth* in that supposed to work?" The answer is given above all in John 6 and 1 Corinthians 11:23–29, which are immensely suggestive in light of Hebrews 10, 12, and 13. In His love for us, Our Lord, having opened the way to heaven through the curtain of His flesh and the price of His blood, imparts them to us in the sacrificial banquet of Holy Communion.

Our final verse to comment on is verse 16:

> 16 And do not forget to do good, and to impart;
> for by **such sacrifices** God's favor is obtained.

This verse captures what Christ Himself did, *par excellence*. "He went about doing good and healing all that were oppressed by the devil, for God was with him" (Act 10:38), and He imparted to us the gifts of grace: "But to every one of us is given grace, according to the measure of the giving of Christ" (Eph 4:7). Our participation in Christ's sacrifice, worthwhile in itself, is meant to bear fruit in our morals, our family life, our social life. We are to imitate Him in doing good and sharing generously with others, because these, too, are sacrifices pleasing to God, by which we obtain His blessing. To put it in more contemporary language, the primary sacrifice is to be understood vertically, as a gift of self to God, to whom we owe everything; but the secondary sacrifice is to be understood horizontally, as a gift of self to neighbor. We are looking at the twin commandment of charity, whereby God is to be loved above all things, with one's whole heart, mind, soul, and strength—our worship should both express this totality and summon it forth from us!—and one's neighbor is to be loved as oneself, for God's sake, and with a view to heavenly beatitude. (As an aside, I find it intriguing that the verse begins: "And do not *forget* to do good...." The Eucharist, which Our Lord instituted as a memorial or commemoration of His supreme act of charity, serves in turn as a mnemonic device or memory aid for us, lest we forget to do for others what Christ has done and is doing for us.)

To summarize, Hebrews 13:10–16 furnishes a portrait of Christian worship. This portrait, like much of the letter, is somewhat veiled: one needs to read between the lines and connect the dots. Christians have an altar from which they eat the one pure, unblemished, all-holy, and all-sufficient sacrifice, in a festal gathering of angels and firstborn sons. We consume the Lamb whose blood sanctifies the people; in this way, we participate in His passion and death, as a foretaste and pledge of immortal life in the city of the heavenly Jerusalem.[19] Our worship is a sacrifice of praise, a work of both Christ and His Church, that sustains us throughout this life of pilgrimage. Like the Incarnate Word and the Church He established, this worship has both an internal, invisible dimension and an external, visible dimension; it is neither an exercise of personal faith alone nor a mere succession of bodily acts performed according to rules, but an exercise of ecclesial faith, verbally expressed, and carried out according to a definite pattern instituted by Christ. This sacrifice of praise models, elicits, and sustains a life of sacrificial love.[20]

It is important to add a caveat or postscript at this point. Prompted by the very text of Hebrews, we have been focusing on the Mass, the Eucharistic sacrifice of praise, but we must not forget that the early Christians themselves continued the Jewish practice of praying at set times throughout the day, as the Acts of the Apostles

---

[19] The mention of illumination and "tasting the heavenly gift" at Hebrews 6:4 is indeed highly suggestive, difficult to sideline as a metaphor, given the known practice of the early Church of admitting the baptized (who were said to be "illuminated") to the banquet of the Eucharist—a practice that has continued without interruption in the Eastern Christian churches.

[20] For an excellent treatment of Hebrews 13 in the context of the Biblical and Patristic teaching on the Eucharist, see Kapler, *Epistle to the Hebrews*, 101–17.

shows us and as records of the apostolic and patristic ages confirm.[21] These regular prayer times, drawing heavily upon the Psalms, were the acorn out of which grew the immense oak tree of the Divine Office, practiced by churches in the cities of the Empire, by the monks in the desert, and finally by the monastic communities that codified the daily and weekly *cursus.* It is not only the Mass that continues the sacrifice of Christ; the Divine Office, the psalmody of the Church, does so as well. Celebrated with faith, devotion, and the involvement of bodily signs of reverence, the Divine Office, too, can be called analogously a *sacrificium laudis* that bears the fruit of God's glorification and man's sanctification. In seamless continuity with the Eucharistic oblation, the solemn psalmody of the Church is an ecclesial participation in the self-offering of Our Lord, an exercise of His eternal high priesthood, a true oblation of rational worship, a pleasing offering to the Most Holy Trinity. By it we are sanctified, transformed into Christ, and conformed to the pattern of the ideal Israel caught up in the heavenly liturgy.

Especially in our times, when the Divine Office has suffered severe textual, ceremonial, and musical impoverishment and has all but disappeared from the lives of so many Catholics, it is crucial to recall, with the Second Vatican Council,[22] that the public liturgy of the Church is

---

[21] The Jews divided the daylight portion of the day into twelve "hours" (cf. Jn 11:9). There were three special hours for prayer: the third, the sixth, and the ninth (cf. Ps 54:18 [55:17]; Dan 6:10). At the third hour, Jesus was crucified (Mk 15:25) and the apostles received the Holy Spirit (Acts 2:15). At the sixth hour, Jesus met the Samaritan woman at the well (Jn 4:6); darkness fell over the earth on Good Friday (Lk 23:44); and Peter, going up to the top of a house to pray, had his vision of the cleansed creation (Acts 10:9). At the ninth hour, Jesus cried out, "My God, My God, why hast Thou forsaken me?" (Mt 27:46; Mk 15:34); Peter and John went up to the temple to pray (Acts 3:1); Cornelius, while praying, had his vision of an angel of God (Acts 10:3).

[22] See the Constitution on the Sacred Liturgy *Sacrosanctum Concilium*, §§ 7–13, 83–85.

made up of far more than the Mass, and that we will tend to overburden the Mass, scramble its content, diminish its peculiar efficacy, and dilute its symbolic expression of the sacrifice of Calvary if we try to make it the sole, all-inclusive, all-sustaining public act of worship that meets every need (real or imagined) of the Christian faithful.[23] Indeed, because the Divine Office is, in a way, more purely an act of loving homage to Almighty God from which we do not stand to "get" anything obvious—there is, in other words, no washing or anointing or absolution or food and drink or other "result" that comes to us, as with the sacraments—it is particularly efficacious in weaning us from subtle or callous forms of pragmatism, activism, and utilitarianism that are so characteristic of our age, typified by the questions "What's in it for me?" and "What good will it do?" When we turn to God again and again, day after day, in the childlike simplicity of a prayer that is of the Word and for the Word, putting His prayers on our lips and making them our own so that we can enter more and more into His inner life, we grow "in wisdom and stature, and in favor with God and man" (cf. Luke 2:52). The virtue of religion is mightily strengthened by this continual offering of praises, thanksgivings, and supplications, for we are, so to speak, burning up our time in a cloud of verbal incense that has no justification for its existence apart from God's worthiness of our attention and our own ineluctable thirst for His life.

The Divine Office, therefore, most perfectly captures the for-itselfness of the *sacrificium laudis* offered by the Church, even as the Holy Mass, being the sacrifice of Christ's very body and blood most perfectly realizes the nature and goal of praise. In this way, the two liturgies require one another for their mutual upbuilding, for the preparation of souls in the art of worship and the

---

[23] On these points, see Peter Kwasniewski, "Lingering in the Courts of the Great King: The Sanctification of Time through Prayer," *The Latin Mass*, vol. 22, n. 1 (Winter/Spring 2013): 14–19.

extension of the Eucharistic mind of Christ into the whole of life. This unity of sacrifice and praise, to which the Church on earth aspires, is the very life of the heavenly city depicted in Hebrews and in the Apocalypse. We see the assembly of the saints offering up prayers and praises before the throne of the Lamb, slain and risen: we see the exemplary worship that is echoed here below in the eightfold psalmody of the Divine Office[24] and made present under a veil in the mystery of the Eucharist. But eye has not seen, nor ear heard, nor the heart of man conceived, what these symbols point to and yet cannot disclose to us pilgrims: the fathomless peace, ineffable joy, and unbounded love awaiting us in the face-to-face vision of God Himself, who is above all praise.

---

[24] Eightfold because of the seven Hours of the daily office plus the night office.

7

Credere oportet accedentem ad Deum: On the Nature and Necessity of Faith

EVAGRIUS HAYDEN, O.S.B.

PROOEMIUM

"Thou hast ascended on high, thou hast led captivity captive; thou hast received gifts in men. Yea for those also that do not believe, the dwelling of the Lord God (Ps 67:19)."

In this verse from the Psalm, the virtue of faith is described for us in all of its four causes, namely material, formal, efficient and final. The material cause is indicated in these words, "Thou hast ascended on high," the formal cause is indicated in the words, "thou hast received gifts in men," the agent cause in the words, "thou hast led captivity captive," and the final cause is indicated in the words, "Yea for those also that do not believe, the dwelling of the Lord God."

The material cause of faith is Christ's ascending on high, for his entering into heaven to intercede on our behalf before the Father is the very object of our belief, or in other words the matter about which is our faith. His ascension is the cause of our salvation, since by his physical absence, space is given for belief. And by believing in the ascension of Christ, we partake in his substance and already begin to participate in that eternal life which is perfected in Him who is our head and to whom it is

necessary that we the members be joined (Heb 3:14). He
is the forerunner and perfecter of our faith who goes to
prepare a place for us (Heb 12:2). Thus it is written, "I
go to prepare a place for you (Jn 14:2)," and again, "he
shall go up opening the way before them . . . and the Lord
at their head (Mich 2:13)."[1]

The formal cause of faith is charity which is an infused
gift of the Holy Spirit.[2] According to another reading it
says "Ascending on high, he led captivity captive: he gave
gifts to men (Eph 4:8)," that is he infuses charity into the
soul of the believer together with the other gifts of the
Holy Spirit. It is by receiving this gift of charity that the
believer in turn becomes as it were a gift to Christ insofar
as they are united to him through love in the bond of
peace (Eph 4:3). Thus the Father gives men to Christ by
infusing them with charity, as it says in the gospel of John,
"I have manifested thy name to the men whom thou hast
given me out of the world (Jn 17:6)." And by this charity
their faith is perfected, that is why he says here, speaking
of Christ, "thou hast received gifts in men."[3]

The agent cause of faith is first of all God moving the
soul through grace, hence the Psalmist says speaking to
God, "thou hast led captivity captive." God by his power
moves and elevates the soul above its nature to believe in
his promise of eternal life "which no eye hath seen nor ear
heard (1 Cor 2:9)." The secondary agent cause of faith is
the will which moves the intellect to assent to that which
it does not see. The will takes the intellect captive, as it
were, and elevates it to be subject to faith in Christ. Hence
the apostle says in another place, "bringing into captivity
every intellect unto the obedience of Christ (1 Cor 10:5)."[4]

---

[1] Thomas Aquinas, *ST* III, q. 57, a. 6, co.
[2] *ST* III, q. 4, a. 3, co.
[3] Thomas Aquinas, *Super Epistula Ad Ephesios*, cap. 4, lect. 3.
[4] Thomas Aquinas, *De Veritate*, in *Quaestiones Disputatae* (Marietti,
1898), q. 14, a. 1, co. Thomas Aquinas, *Commentarium in Boetium
de Trinitate* (Marietti, 1898), q. 2, a. 3, co.

The proximate final cause of faith is first of all to confound unbelievers, hence he says "Yea for those also that do not believe." The faith of Christians is a stumbling block and a proof against those who deny the authority of Christ and prefer to "lean upon their own prudence (Prov 3:5)." But the ultimate cause and final purpose of faith is to bring the just into the heavenly dwelling of the Lord to be with him for eternity. And this is indicated in the words, "the dwelling of the Lord God."

Let us therefore enter into this mystery, and so seeking let us try to understand the substance and foundation of faith upon which rests the whole purpose and end of our life here on earth. Let us seek to unfold its nature and definition, and finally try to understand why it is so necessary for us in order to be saved and attain to eternal life. In my examination of the nature and necessity of faith, I will use as my sources several works of St. Thomas Aquinas, the primary ones being his treatise on faith in the *De Veritate*, his treatise on the same in the *Secunda Secundae* of the *Summa Theologica*, and his commentary on the *De Trinitate* of Boethius. My mode of procedure will be to use arguments from reason by which I will seek to manifest through likenesses and analogies that which we hold as authoritative and as revealed by God through the writings of St. Paul.

THE NATURE OF FAITH

Belief: the Act of Faith

I will first seek to unfold the nature of faith, after which I will examine its necessity. Now, in order to see what is the nature of faith, we must first lay out what it means to believe, that is, what is the act of faith. Belief is always with regards to something that is held to be true, for people do not believe in that which they hold to be false. But the true and false are properly about affirmations and denials which the intellect composes. Thus the act of faith will properly be in the intellect.

That is why the act of faith, taken generally, is defined
by Aquinas and Augustine as "to think with assent." By
the word "to think," belief is set apart from the first act
of the intellect called "simple apprehension" by which it
knows the simple essences of things. This means then that
belief is about composed statements that are either true
or false. And this thinking in belief is said to be together
"with assent" because the thinking of the intellect does
not come before the assent causing the intellect to adhere
to the proposition as true, as happens in knowledge and
understanding where one reduces the proposition to first
principles which are clearly seen. In belief the intellect is
moved to assent to the believable proposition solely by
the motion of the will.[5] Because the intellect is moved
to this assent by the command of the will, and not by
the evidence of its proper object, thus the assent of the
intellect will be blind, for it is coerced to assent by principles which are foreign to its vision.[6]

The Definition of Faith According to Aquinas
1. *Different Kinds of Faith*
Given then that the act of belief is "to think with
assent," let us know seek to derive a definition of the
disposition of faith itself, from which the act of belief
arises. This disposition from which arises the act of belief
and "makes the intellect to assent to that which is not
seen"[7] is what we call the habit of faith in the common
sense. However, there are two different species of faith,
according to the two different ways that the object of the
intellect is not seen, on the one hand on account of a
defect in the thing itself insofar it is a contingent thing
or distant physically from us and therefore removed from
our sense experience, or on the other hand it is not seen
on account of a defect in us insofar as the thing exceeds

---

[5] Aquinas, *ST* II-II, q. 2, a. 1, co.
[6] Aquinas, *De Veritate*, q. 14, a. 1, co.
[7] Aquinas, *ST* II-II, q. 4, a. 1, co.

our power of knowledge, as in divine and eternal things.[8] Regarding the former one would have natural faith, by which one man believes the testimony of another man regarding what is absent from him by place or time. Regarding the latter one would have the virtue of theological faith properly so called by which one believes God himself regarding things that are unable to be seen by the intellect simply speaking and not only with respect to place or time. We know generally that theological faith is something in the soul, like a habit or a disposition, and furthermore that it involves in some way God and the things that God reveals as its object. Like human faith which has as its object the testimony and promises of other men and confides in them because it seems fitting or useful, faith which has God as its object confides in the testimony of God and the promises that he makes to man.

2. Principle of Belief in the Will

Now, since there are two powers of the soul involved in the act of belief, namely intellect and will, for the will is what moves the intellect to believe, then there must be two principles to the act of belief, that is, a disposition in each of these powers of the soul by which the believer can be said to have the habit of faith, a habit which disposes him to more readily believe when he wishes.

Regarding the principle or disposition of belief that is in the will, since the will has as its proper object the desirable good and the final end, thus the disposition by which the will is moved in the act of faith will also regard the desirable good and final end. Thus it is the goodness of the end that ultimately moves the believer to assent to faith. The will is only moved by its own proper object which is the universal good, and by the particular goods that fall under it. But for man there are two final ends, one that is proportionate to nature and the other that exceeds nature.

---

[8] Aquinas, *In Boetium de Trinitate*, q. 3, a. 1, co.

The good of man and the end that is proportionate to nature is the happiness which Aristotle speaks of in book 1 of the *Ethics*. This happiness consists both in an active life of virtue guided by prudence, and also a contemplative life ordered towards wisdom and knowing the causes of things. Every man is capable of attaining this dual happiness since it is commensurate with human nature, for every man has an intrinsic ordering to this end given that they have a soul equipped with reason with an intellect that is both practical and theoretical.

And yet, there is another end of man that exceeds human nature, namely the knowledge and enjoyment of the vision of God. This end lies outside our capabilities, comprehension, and desire, for one cannot desire what they do not know, and the vision of God is in no way proportioned to our mode of knowing which comes through the senses. And yet every man possesses an immediate ordering to this supernatural end. He alone of all bodily creatures has immediate knowledge of created universal being and goodness, since these are both the proper objects of his intellect and will. And thus nothing can truly quench man's thirst for knowledge or quiet his desire for happiness except to comprehend the highest truth and to attain the greatest good, which are both found in God alone.[9] Thus man naturally desires eternal life and to participate in God's life and knowledge of Himself. And yet this eternal life is something that exceeds man's natural powers. Thus he must depend upon the divine liberality to make the attainment of eternal life possible. Therefore it is from seeing this good of eternal life that is promised by God in divine revelation that the will begins to desire and is inclined to assent to that which it does not yet see, and it is moved thus to believe that God will be faithful to his promise of eternal life.

Now, in order for the will to desire anything, the thing desired must already begin to be in the appetite

---

[9] Aquinas, *ST* I-II, q. 2, a. 8, co.; II-II, q. 2, a. 3 co.

according to a certain proportion. This is because in order for something to be desired, it must first be known by the one desiring, at least in a general and obscure way. And therefore the object of desire must already exist in the intellect intentionally, and it must be impressed in the will as a kind of connatural inclination. Thus the end that is desired begins to be already in the will in the mode of a certain likeness or imitation. That is why, as Aquinas says, in faith "there comes to be in human nature a certain *beginning* of the good itself which is proportionate to nature."[10] He says again in his commentary on Ephesians, "Faith is a beginning of that future understanding, because it is the substance of things to be hoped for, . . . as if it makes those things to be hoped for to subsist in us now in the mode of a certain beginning."[11]

Thus, we can say that the desire of the will that moves the intellect to believe is already a beginning of that eternal life which it hopes to have fully one day in the vision of God.

3. Principle of Belief in the Intellect

Now let us talk about the other principle of faith that is in the intellect. Since the intellect is immediately ordered towards the object of its understanding, not as the thing exists in itself, that is outside the intellect, but as received into itself as an intelligible species, thus it is necessary that the intellect receive or assent to the thing understood according to its own intelligible mode. But the proper mode by which the intellect receives or assents to anything is insofar as it is moved directly by the object of the understanding. And this only happens when the object of understanding is clearly seen and manifestly reduced to self evident first principles. When this is the case, the intellect is moved by nature to assent to the understood object as something true.

---

[10] Aquinas, *De Veritate*, q. 14, a. 2, co.
[11] Aquinas, *Super Ep. ad Ephesios*, cap. 3, lect. 5.

Now, the intellect can be moved not only by its own proper object and according to its own mode, but also by the subject itself, that is by the will which coerces the intellect to act in a mode that is foreign or superior to its own proper mode. The will, in this case, moves the intellect to assent to principles that are not seen by the intellect nor knowable with respect to us, but they are known through themselves and clearly seen by a foreign science, such as by the knowledge of another man who bears witness to something distant from our immediate experience, or else they are known by a higher science, such as by the knowledge that the saints and angels have of God, or the knowledge that He has of himself. But, not being a knowledge that is proper or proportionate to our intellect, the intellect is thus forced by the will to assent to something as true which it does not yet see as true. That is why the intellect is said to be blind in its assent, since it adheres to that which does not appear.

4. Participation in God's Knowledge of Himself

Although the intellect in the virtue of faith is blind simply speaking, it nonetheless has a true participation in God's knowledge and vision of Himself. Let us try to understand this more deeply. In order to see how we can participate in God's knowledge of Himself through faith, we must first ask, how God knows Himself. Since God is utterly uncompounded and simple, therefore God's very act of understanding is identical with his essence. And therefore God's very nature is to know Himself. And, since He is the first truth and the source of all truth, thus God's knowledge of himself is for his own sake. And it is through knowing his own essence that He in turn knows all creatures that proceed from him. God, in knowing Himself, sees all the actual and possible ways that His being can be participated in creatures, just as any one who comprehends fully the power of a cause can see all the ways that its power can be participated in its effects.

Because every effect imitates its cause in some way, and since Man is created by God, thus he will imitate his Creator, although in an imperfect mode. We can say then that the way God knows Himself will be similar to the way Man knows God, but imperfectly. Thus, we can make a proportion and say that just as God knows all things first of all through knowing His own being and substance as first cause and principle of creatures, so also does the intellect of the believer know through assenting to the substance and foundation of faith all the conclusions that follow on and build upon those first fundamental principles of faith. And the first principle of faith is, according to St. Paul, to "believe that God exists and is a rewarder to them that seek him (Heb 11:6)." And thus, by assenting to this first principle of faith, one adheres to all the other articles of faith which flow from it. And in the light of that first principle, basic substance and foundation of faith the believer sees all other conclusions that derive from it as being true.

Faith also imitates and participates in God's knowledge of himself insofar as by faith the believer adheres to God for His own sake. Just as God knows Himself for His own sake as the first truth by which all other things are true, so also does the believer through faith that is infused in his soul assent and adhere to the first truth which is God Himself, for His own sake and by whom all other things are true.[12]

Furthermore, just as God's knowledge is absolutely certain and firm, so faith, although blind, will share in God's certain and necessary knowledge of Himself. That is why in Hebrews St. Paul says not only that it is of things not seen, but that it is the "argument" or "conviction of things not seen (Heb 11:1)." By this word "conviction" St. Paul indicates the certainty and the firm adhesion of the understanding to the first truth in faith.[13] But this certainty is not that which one has in demonstrative

---

[12] Aquinas, *In Boetium de Trinitate*, q. 2, a. 2, co.
[13] Aquinas, *ST* II-II, q. 4, a. 1.

knowledge, as we've seen, for that certainty comes from a reduction to self-evident first principles, which cannot be had in faith. Rather the certainty in faith comes from the will. This lack of vision in faith however is not the same as that which is had in doubt, suspicion or opinion, for in neither of these three is their any firm assent or conviction. Rather, faith is in the middle between the vision and certainty of knowledge on the one hand and the blindness and uncertainty of doubt on the other, sharing something in common with each of them.

Given then what we have discovered in this general exposition of the two objects of faith, that in the will and that in the intellect, we can now draw forth certain marks which, when taken together, supply us with all that we need to make a definition. Since faith is principally in the intellect, for it is the intellect which gives the assent, thus we say that it is "a habit of the mind," by which is indicated the genus of faith. And yet since it has two objects, one in the intellect and one in the will, our definition will have to take into account both of these. With regard to the object of faith that is in the will, we say it is that "by which eternal life is begun in us" since it is a beginning of the knowledge that God has of Himself, and which we will have in the beatific vision. But with regard to the object that is in the intellect we say that faith "makes the intellect to assent to that which does not appear." Thus faith as defined by Aquinas is "a habit of the mind by which eternal life is begun in us making the intellect to assent to that which does not appear."[14]

THE NECESSITY OF FAITH
Kinds of Necessity

Having laid out in detail the nature of faith according to St. Thomas Aquinas, now I will turn to the second part of my lecture and try to understand why faith is necessary.

---

[14] Aquinas, *De Veritate*, q. 14, a. 2, co.

We can prove this first of all from authority, taking the subtitle of this lecture as our argument: St. Paul says in chapter 11 of Hebrews that "it is necessary that the one drawing near to God believe... (Heb 11:6)." But let us try to unpack this statement so as to better grasp this necessity of belief. We must first then understand what it means for something to be necessary. Now, something can be said to be necessary when it is not able not to be. In other words, it must be. But this necessity can said in different ways.[15] Something is necessary either from an intrinsic principle of its own being, such as it being necessary that any incorruptible being continue to exist, or that a triangle have interior angles equal to two rights, and this we call "natural" or "absolute" necessity. Or else something is necessary from an extrinsic principle of its being, such as from the agent who "coerces" the thing to be. And from this we have necessity "of constraint." Or it is necessary on account of the "end" and "purpose" whose fulfillment is required for the completion of the act. And from this we have necessity "of the end." And this final kind of necessity can be either an absolute necessity where the end is supplied by nature, such as it being necessary that every man desire happiness universally, or else it can be necessary by supposition such that, given a supposed end not supplied directly by nature but being either below, exceeding, or proportionate to nature, something else would follow from that assumed end necessarily as a consequence.[16]

That Faith is Necessary

1. Necessity of Natural Faith

Now, in order to understand how faith is necessary for man, we must look first of all at man himself and apply each of these kinds of necessity to him and see which ones pertain to his act of faith. If we take faith as the

---

[15] Aquinas, *ST* I, q. 82, a. 1, co.
[16] Thomas Aquinas, *In Libros Sententiarum*, IV, d. 7, q. 1, a. 1b, co.

natural virtue which has the testimony of another man as
its object, then there seems here to be a certain necessity
that arises from man's natural end of desiring happiness.
And since this end is common to all by nature, thus it
seems to carry something of absolute necessity with it. It is
universally true and natural that all children believe their
parents when they are young. And furthermore it is true
that all men have some basic faith in others, and in turn
seek to speak the truth even to strangers and assume in
good faith that others will speak the truth to themselves.

A. *According to Man's End of Active Virtue.* The reason for
the natural reciprocal trust between men is that since they
are by nature rational beings they seek to live together
in a society so as to live better and more efficiently and
thus attain happiness more securely. Man's natural end
which is a happiness that is according to reason is only
attained by living a life of virtue, and yet many virtues
are only able to be attained by living in community with
other men, such as the virtues of justice, friendship, or
love of neighbor. Thus there is a certain necessity built
into the very nature of man to live with others. But there
can be no association of men in a city or a nation if there
is not some agreement and faith between them. Faith
is the foundation of all justice and in fact of all spoken
truth. That is why, as Aquinas says, every lie is a sin, for
there is no lie which does not derogate from this faith
which is so necessary to human concourse.[17] From this
then we can conclude that with regard to man's natural
end ordered towards the active life of virtue and of living
well in a society, there is a certain absolute necessity to
have faith in other men.

B. *According to Man's End of Contemplative Virtue.* There
is also a necessity of faith that arises from man's natural
end that is for the contemplation of wisdom. In order
to attain wisdom one needs to learn from others the
sciences and arts that lead to and prepare the way for

---

[17] Aquinas, *In Boetium de Trinitate*, q. 3, a. 1, co.

wisdom. Children learn from their parents first of all by imitating their actions, and then later on by listening to their words. Likewise a student learns from his teacher either by imitating him in the case of learning an art, or else by listening to his doctrine in the case of learning a theoretical science. In both cases the child or student is first of all in a state of imperfect knowledge, but then is led by the one instructing him to a state of perfect knowledge. But no teacher reveals all of the most subtle reasons to his student right from the beginning, rather he first gives him some imperfect knowledge whose reasons and arguments he keeps hidden which are later to be revealed to him more perfectly and in depth. But until the student arrives at full knowledge of the causes and principles of the science which he is learning, he must assume these from his teacher as true, and thus it is necessary by nature for the student to believe his teacher. Otherwise he could not even begin to arrive at perfect knowledge.[18]

This necessity of faith with respect to man's natural end of contemplation of wisdom is also seen in the order of the sciences. Metaphysics, or the science of wisdom which is about the highest causes and in which is proved the principles and foundation of all knowledge, is nevertheless learned only after all the other sciences have been completed. Hence the name, μετα-φυσική, after the physics, indicates that the study of "being as being" only comes after the study of "natural being." And yet in all the subalternated sciences, such as mathematics or physics, certain preambles and principles are assumed which are only fully understood at the very end, when one studies them in depth in the science of metaphysics. For example, according to the principle of identity of being in metaphysics, the same thing is the same with itself, and when that principle is assumed by the science of mathematics, it becomes the principle of equality such that quantities equal to the same quantity are equal to

---

[18] Aquinas, *De Veritate*, q. 14, a. 10.

each other. In the subalternate science of mathematics, the principle of identity of quantity is received and
believed as true based on the testimony of the higher
science of metaphysics, because it cannot be proved by
the science of mathematics itself, and yet it can be proved
by the higher science to which it is subject. And thus
any one studying a subalternate science must first of all
assume and believe the principles which are only later on
proved in the higher architectonic science.[19] Thus, from
the foregoing we can see that there is a certain necessity
for natural faith given the final end of happiness which
is in all men, whether that happiness be pursued according to a life of active virtue or else according to a life of
contemplation ordered towards wisdom.

    C. *According to the Agent of Faith (The Will)*. Now there
is another kind of necessity pertaining to natural faith
that arises from the will of man himself. We spoke above
regarding the necessity of constraint that arises from the
agent moving the patient to do or suffer something. In our
definition of faith given above, we saw that the will in the
act of faith moves the intellect to adhere to that which is
not seen and thus "to think with assent." The will is able
to move the intellect and coerce it to assent with certainty
because it is the first mover of all the other powers in the
soul. The intellect, since it lies under the power of the will,
is thus constrained to assent to something with certainty,
because the will commands it to do so. The intellect, as
said above, is not moved sufficiently by the object itself of
belief, because it does not see it as being reduced to first
principles which are seen and known through themselves.
But the will on the other hand is moved sufficiently by
the object of belief because although it does not see it
as reduced to first principles, nonetheless it is drawn by
the goodness, fittingness and usefulness of the object of
belief. Thus, even though the intellect is constrained to
assent by the necessity imposed on it by the will, yet the

---

[19] Aquinas, *In Boetium de Trinitate*, q. 3, a. 1, co.

act of belief is still completely free and thus a completely human act. The will is only ever infallibly moved by its own proper object which is the universal good, to which it cannot help but be drawn. But the will is nevertheless completely free and undetermined to pursue or avoid the particular goods which are presented to it as the material objects of belief. And it will make its choice of whether to consent or not to any particular belief depending on how it presents the object of belief to itself, either under the aspect of good or bad. If good, then the will is drawn towards it and moves the intellect to assent. If bad, then the will does not coerce the intellect to assent. Nevertheless such a necessity of constraint does not mean that the will cannot err in its judgment of whether the object of belief is truly good, or only an apparent good.

With the supernatural virtue of faith that has God as its object, the necessity of constraint from the agency of the will does indeed move the intellect infallibly to assent, because it does so under the formal aspect of this object of belief being revealed by God. And it furthermore consents to the material object of belief, that is the proposition itself of belief, which is infallibly true insofar as it has been revealed by God himself who cannot lie. And yet, even if the will assent to a belief which it thinks is true as having been revealed by God, it might happen that the material object of belief has not in fact been revealed by God. In this case the faith is false, and more to be called "human estimation" since, in order to be true, faith requires both the proper formal object, assented to as revealed by God, and the proper material object, that which God actually reveals.

And even if both the material and formal object of belief are present, it doesn't mean that at some time in the future the will might loosen its hold on the intellect and allow it to stop assenting to what it believed before. Since the object of supernatural faith is only participated by the intellect imperfectly in this life so that it does not

see the truth of the proposition, thus it is left to continue
reasoning and seeks to ground the object of belief in first
principles, even though it cannot. And yet, despite this
wandering-about of the intellect, it being unable to stop
its discourse of reason even though subject to the command of assent by the will, the will nevertheless is completely at rest in its belief, so long as it chooses to see the
object of belief as something good and worthy of assent.

2. *Necessity of Supernatural Faith*

A. *That Man learns from God by Revelation.* We've spoken then of the necessity arising from an end supplied
by nature and that arising from the agent itself. Now, a
third kind of necessity arises in the act of belief if we suppose that there is a final end of man that exceeds nature,
namely to know God face to face. Given then that man has
God as his final supernatural end, man would of necessity
depend upon God in order to attain this end. The reason
for this is that every motion depends upon its final term
in order to exist, for there cannot be any motion unless it
be towards some end and goal. Thus, if there is a motion
and operation proper to man which has the supernatural
knowledge of God as its final goal, then for man to even
begin to reason and to contemplate, he must depend upon
God who is the final goal, end and perfection of his very
act of reasoning. The philosopher Heraclitus gives us a
proportion that illustrates this dependency of man upon
God: "A man [like an] infant gives ear to God, just as a
child gives ear to a man (ἀνὴρ νήπιος ἤκουσε πρὸς δαίμονος
ὅκωσπερ παῖς πρὸς ἀνδρός)."[20] This fragment of Heraclitus
can be restated in the form of a 3 term proportion: as a
child is to a man, so is a man to God.

This relation between man and God can be expressed
both with regards to man's very being which he receives
from God, and also with regards to man's knowledge by
which he learns from God. As a child is generated from a

---

[20] Heraclitus, Fragmenta (0626:002), in *Die Fragmente Der Vorsokra-
tiker*, ed. Diels, 6th ed., vol. 1 (Weidmann, 1951), fragment 77, line 1.

man and is made in his father's image and likeness, even though at birth he completely lacks any act of reason, so also is man generated by God and carries the image of a rational soul in himself by which he is in the image and likeness of God even though infinitely below the dignity of God's intellect. Likewise with regards to knowledge, with respect to this proportion of Heraclitus, we can see that as a child learns from a man so does a man learn from God. But, a child learns from his father first of all by imitating him, and then later on by listening to his words and to those of other men. So likewise does a man learn from God first of all by contemplating his imitations and the traces that he has left in creatures, but later on he learns from God's words themselves, that is by listening to his inspirations and divine revelation.[21]

If indeed man's final end is the knowledge of God, then it is necessary that he learn from God not only through sensible creation, but also from God revealing himself to man through intelligible words, as Heraclitus indicated; for there are many things regarding God's nature that exceed our natural capacities. And this is clear from the fact that man can only learn in this life through the senses. And thus he will only ascertain those effects of God which can be perceived through sense, such as motion, order, and causality, all of which point to the fact that God exists. But in no way can man learn from sensible creation regarding God's actions ad intra, nor discern the nature of God as to what He is. Creation, being an effect that is not equal to its cause, only participates in God's being in a very partial way, and thus can only declare a small portion of his nature.[22] And so, if man's final and supernatural end is to see God as He is, that is to behold his very nature, then it is necessary that God reveal himself to man first.

---

[21] I owe this analogy to a lecture by Duane Berquist.
[22] Thomas Aquinas, *Summa Contra Gentiles*, Book I, trans. Fathers of the English Dominican Province (New York: Benzinger Brothers, 1924), cap. 3.

B. That the Soul is Moved by God in Faith. To have faith, however, it is not only necessary that God reveal himself to man, but also that He move the soul to believe in that which he has revealed. In order to see this necessity, we must first of all see how it is possible at all that man can be moved by God to have faith in something that exceeds his natural capabilities. The reason for this is that wherever there is an order between two distinct natures that have a relation of greater to lesser, for example between man and God, the lower nature will always be completed and perfected both by its own proper motion, which would be a natural motion, as well as by the motion of the higher nature in its regard, which would be a supernatural motion.[23] In the case of man, since he possesses a rational soul, thus he is ordered to the universal principal of all being, namely God himself, and by this ordering to God, he is thus able to be moved by God above his own nature. The reason for this is that the rational soul apprehends naturally the universal account of created being. Universal being is the very first thing that falls into the intellect, and it is by this universal account of being that all other things are apprehended by the intellect. But this very same natural ordering of the rational soul to apprehend the universal account of being comes from God himself, for He is both the principle of created universal being, and the very cause of the existence of the soul.[24] Thus, there is an immediate ordering between the lower rational creature and God its Creator. Therefore we can say that if the rational creature can be moved by its own natural motion to apprehend the universal account of being while here in this life, all the more can it be moved by a motion above its nature and proper to God, to apprehend Himself, the principle of all being, by a certain participation in His divine goodness.

   Now, although it is possible that man be moved to apprehend the principle of universal being, that is God

---

[23] Aquinas, *ST* II-II, q. 2, a. 3.
[24] *ST* I-II, q. 114, a.1.

Himself, based on man's immediate ordering to that apprehension, man cannot in any way move himself to this end since this is wholly above his natural faculties. Thus he must learn gradually from God as from a teacher who reveals the truth, or as a helpless child in the arms of its mother. If any child must trust its mother who coddles him or any student trust its teacher who educates him to attain his natural end of virtue and wisdom, all the more must man trust God and believe in him so as to learn of his last and supernatural end, and how to attain it. Thus the act of faith is necessary for salvation according to man's supernatural end of seeing God face to face.

C. *That Man Moves Himself in Faith.* I have spoken of the necessity that God reveals himself in faith and that He move the soul in a supernatural way to believe. Now I will touch briefly, before closing, on the necessity that the soul also move itself freely to believe. This necessity is based on the supposition that man gain his salvation by his own meritorious act.

If God wished, he could simply give man the gift of the beatific vision without any merit on man's part. But supposing that God deals with man according to the tenets of commutative justice, then there is a fittingness and a certain necessity that man be able to earn his eternal reward by his own act. It is more in consonance with the dignity of God's sublime nature as first cause and Lord of the universe that he work through secondary causes to attain his purposes, just as a king operates in his own kingdom and court by means of many intermediary and subordinate agents. Thus, assuming that God desires to accomplish man's salvation according to a greater fittingness, then it follows that man should be allowed a part and agency in his own salvation as a secondary cause accomplishing the dictates of God and earning the reward which God desires to give him.

Now, any act that comes from man can only be said to be proper to him insofar as it proceeds from reason, for by this power he is distinguished from all other mate-rial creatures. But, the fact that an act is done by reason is not enough to make it a meritorious act, for merit carries with it the act of a free will, while that which is done under constraint of another or by nature cannot be said to be merited or free. And yet, the act of reason whereby the intellect consents to principles that are seen and manifest through themselves is not free and thus not meritorious, for the intellect is moved to such a consent by nature and not by the will.

On the other hand, the act of faith whereby the will, interiorly moved by grace, moves the intellect in turn to assent to divine truth, is itself an entirely free act, for any act of man is free and human insofar as it proceeds from a will undetermined by nature or external force. Thus, since the act of faith moved by interior grace is a wholly free act, then it also meritorious. And thus, assuming that God only rewards according to merit, then it is necessary that man have faith in order to attain eternal life.[25]

CONCLUSION

In this lecture I have sought to explain both what is faith and why it is necessary.

In order to understand the nature of faith, first I looked at the act of belief, which is defined as "to think with assent." I then examined the definition of faith according to Aquinas which was "a habit of the mind by which eternal life is begun in us making the intellect to assent to that which does not appear."

In the second part of the lecture I sought to manifest why faith is necessary by looking first of all at three dif-ferent senses of the word "necessary," namely that accord-ing to nature or else absolute necessity, that according to the agent or else necessity by constraint, and finally necessity according to the end or by supposition. I then applied these different kinds of necessity first of all to

---

[25] *ST* II-II, q. 2, a. 9, co.

natural faith that has the testimony of other men as its object. We saw that there is a natural necessity for faith that follows from man's end of living according to virtue and the contemplation of truth. We also saw that there is a necessity by constraint that arises from man's will itself in the act of natural faith.

After looking at the necessity of natural faith we then looked at supernatural faith which relies on the testimony of God and saw that, supposing that man has a final end that exceeds his natural capabilities, namely the vision of God, it is necessary that man have supernatural faith in order to achieve his end. We also saw how the soul in the supernatural act of faith is moved by God above its nature to believe, and that man can still be said to move himself in faith, allowing him to merit the promised reward of eternal life.

By faith then let us hold fast the confession of our hope (Heb 10:23). Through faith and hope we ascend on high with Christ until we arrive at that dwelling of the Lord God of which the psalmist speaks (Ps 67:19). Let our faith then give birth to praise so that, like the psalmist we might say, "Sing ye to God, Who mounteth above the heaven of heavens, to the east… God is wonderful in his saints: the God of Israel is he who will give power and strength to his people. Blessed be God" (Ps 67:34, 36).

8

Christ as Head of the Human Race

DANIEL LENDMAN

I TAKE AS MY INSPIRATION FOR THIS talk Aquinas's words at the end of the commentary: "Short talks are most welcome; for if they are good they are heard eagerly, and if they are bad they grieve little." And he quotes the Scripture from Ecclesiasticus, "Let your words be few." There are many reasons a talk can be bad, and I won't go into all of those; but one of the reasons a talk can be bad is that it can be in error, and a brief reflection on this will help set our theme.

Correct speech about things is very difficult, especially when we try to become more determinate about things, and speak more precisely about things. This is true enough for natural things, close to our experience (Aquinas remarks somewhere that we can't even express the essence of a fly or a gnat), but it's also true of those things that are more removed from our experience and sensation. Thus, with regard to metaphysics, it is very hard to speak correctly about things that are so removed from us in our day to day experience, at least according to our senses. In theology, however, we propose to do something — *audemus*, we dare to do something — that is even beyond this. We're not simply speaking of things that are beyond our senses and beyond our experience, or things that we've reasoned to. In this science, we try to speak about things that transcend the power of reason itself. These things are mysteries, they go beyond our reason in their *superintelligibility*, in the brilliance of the mystery that is presented to us. And but for revelation, to dare to talk about these sorts of things would be a task for fools and poets alone.

Now, in theology we can make a division of the kinds of mysteries revealed to us. There are those mysteries that seem to be utterly transcendent in the sense that they are wholly beyond our reason and wholly beyond our experience: the Holy Trinity is such a mystery. No mind would ever have posited a Trinity in any sort of authoritative way, or even by way of conjecture, were it not for revelation. Another kind of mystery that we are confronted with arises because of the Incarnation, and that is when the absolutely transcendent, God himself, has somehow become concrete. Thus, because of the Incarnation, had we been in Palestine about two thousand years ago, we could have pointed to a true man, and said, "There is God; this one, there, is God." And there is still another kind of mystery, wherein it is not simply hidden from our senses or beyond our reason, but it's actually an affront to our senses as well as being beyond reason. This is realized in the Eucharist, where we hold up something that looks, tastes, feels like bread, and we say, "This is the body of Christ." This might be at least *a* reason for why we call the Eucharist the *mysterium fidei*; a sort of mystery *par excellence*. (There are other reasons too.)

Why all of this discussion of mystery? Well, in this talk it is the second class of mystery of which I will speak. Thus, in this lecture we're dealing with the fact that the utterly transcendent God has become man; or more precisely, has taken human nature unto himself. There are many things that are a consequence of the Incarnation, and I am going to argue that one of them is that, in virtue of the Incarnation, it follows that Christ is the natural head over all mankind. By "natural" here, I mean that it follows from His very nature, who He is, that He is head of mankind and that he has authority over us as head according to nature. This would be distinct, then, especially from the order of grace, but we'll talk about that more as we go on. In this sort of mystery, then, we will be attempting to articulate something that goes beyond what reason and our senses can know. We must rely upon Revelation. Further, we must rely upon what is implied by Revelation to bring out this otherwise obscure doctrine.

The order of the talk is as follows: I shall first discuss headship in general, then headship over the Church; headship over all mankind; and then we shall conclude.

HEADSHIP IN GENERAL

In order to speak correctly about headship we must remember that when we use the word "head," we use the word in many ways and we're applying it in all these different ways by way of analogy. That means that there is a first and proper way of using the term, and that we can properly apply it to different things because of a certain resemblance to that first use of the term. First of all, then, when we use the term, "head" we're talking about the head of an animal, typically; most excellently, the head of a man. That's the first meaning of it. All the other senses of the term extend from this first use. In the first use of the term, if you speak of a head, then it implies that there's a body, and a living body. A living body is organized and united, operating according to a single principle, a principle of life that in living things we call the soul.

Now when we extend the term, "head" to name other things, some of those characteristics that belonged to the first use of the name change. So when we talk about the CEO of a corporation being "head" of a corporation, that's a real sense of "head," but it's an analogous sense. We (of course) wouldn't say that a corporation has a soul, but it does have perhaps some uniting principle by which the whole operates, and this can be understood analogously as the "life" of the corporation (maybe their mission statement or their plan or whatever). The whole of the corporation is, then, united in this and operates according to this principle. Leading the whole corporation, though, is the CEO, who gives it direction, and determines what sort of corporation it will be, to a large extent. He is the *head* of the corporation. Thus, we see there are ways in which we can extend the term. What is essential, however, is that the head is always seen as the principal part and the principle of the life of the body. It is the most important and most essential aspect of the body in many ways. (I don't want to get into a head vs. heart dispute here.)

In the Third Part of St. Thomas Aquinas's *Summa Theologiae*, Question 8, Article 3 he is treating Christ's headship over all mankind. Here he argues to Christ's universal headship through His headship over the Church. Now, when Thomas is identifying what it is to be head, he notes three essential characteristics that belong to every head, and these are order, perfection, and power. He argues this by looking to the way order, perfection, and power are held in a natural head. He argues that the head is the first part of the body and it is the principle of the order of the body, and it gives order to the rest of the body. Secondly, the head is said to have perfection. Why? Because, as Thomas argues, it's the seat of all the senses: sight, hearing, taste, smelling, touch; all of them are in the head. In the rest of the body, however, there is only touch. So there's a certain kind of perfection in the head; it possesses all of the perfections of the whole of the body in itself. Then he argues that the head is the seat of power because it's the head that, as it were, gives direction to the rest of the body. You go here or there according to the knowledge that you have (and here I'm just talking sense knowledge). So the order gives rise to the perfection, because it's the first in the body; and these both give rise to its power over the rest of the body.

With this natural understanding of what it is to be a head, we can then go on to see how the meaning of head is expressed and realized in other extended senses, and first in Christ's headship over the Church.

HEADSHIP OVER THE CHURCH

The headship over the Church that belongs to Christ means that he is the principle of order in the Church; he is the perfection of the Church; and he has power over the whole of the Church. This might be something very easy for us to assent to. It seems fitting that Christ would be head and have all these things. But it behooves us to explore the reasoning that Thomas gives us particularly in order to see what's behind this and see how we might be able to extend this notion of headship in other ways.

Thomas argues for Christ's headship over the Church through the order of grace. So the headship over the Church is according to grace. So, if Christ is going to be called head of the Church, he must have these aspects of order, perfection, and power according to the order of grace. I think it's easy enough, but it's worth saying that Christ is the principle of grace for all others. There is no grace that comes to the world, to any of us in the world, outside of Christ. And this arises because of his Incarnation. As Thomas argues, it's because of the proximity of his human nature to God. And this is an important understanding about what is in the mindset of Thomas when he's talking about this, where he sees creation as a kind of mediated thing, where you have God, and then angels, and man, etc., so God's operations are kind of mediated to the rest of the world, to the rest of creation. This is true in the natural order of things, but this is also true according to the supernatural order, the order of grace. And God's grace is mediated not principally through angels but, as Thomas is pointing out here, through Christ; from God through Christ's human nature, to and through our Lady, through the Church, and to the rest of the world. So also Christ has the perfection of all grace. And Thomas argues for this by saying, quoting John 1, "We have seen him full of grace and truth." And there Thomas understands the words "full of grace" in the sense that he has the absolute perfection of grace, and not as having received it but as being the source of all grace. And so also he has power in the sense that he has the power to infuse grace into all of us. And this is according to the Scripture, "From his fullness we have all received." Therefore, Thomas concludes, Christ can validly be called head over all the Church.

But remember what we said in the beginning. Head implies body. In order for there to be a head, there has to be a body. So in order for Christ to be said to be head over the Church, it presupposes that there has to be a body of the Church. And this, of course, is the case. We have the great theology of the body of Christ that St. Paul gives us, probably most explicitly, in his First Letter to the Corinthians. There is in fact one body of Christ, of which all the members are united to Christ in grace. But Thomas goes further. He says, even in virtue of this order of grace, Christ can be said to be head over *all* mankind. This is a wonder. How is it possible that Christ is head of all mankind according to the order of grace, if in fact not all men are united to Christ in grace?

Thomas breaks it down, saying Christ is head over all mankind according to this order of grace, but in diverse ways. And he's going to lay out five ways. The first is that he is head of, and so is united with: those who are in glory with him. This is referring, of course, to those in heaven, the Church triumphant. Secondly, he is head and he is united with those who are in a state of charity. This would refer to the Church suffering and to those who are in a state of grace in the Church militant. Thirdly, he is head to those who are united to him in faith. If I understand him correctly, he is talking about those with unformed faith. This would be those in the Church militant who have fallen out of the state of grace, those who have lost the life of charity in their soul. Then, there is the last two, which are kind of different than the preceding three. The first is those that are united to him in potency. (And potency is a loaded term in some ways. It means a lot. It has a lot of connotations in scholastic theology. It's a term that's taken over from

Aristotle.) Thomas argues that Christ is head, indeed, over those who are united to him potentially in grace; that is, those who are not now united to him according to grace either through faith or through charity, but will be at some point in the future. Finally he argues there is also a fifth type, those who are not now united to him in grace but never shall be. So those are the five possibilities.

Now you can look at this and just see in it a very dry scholastic approach: dividing into all the logical possibilities and there is nothing much more to that. But I think there is more to it. And I think there might be more in this idea of potency, this idea of being potentially united to Christ as head even according to the order of grace. What I'm going to suggest now is that this potency indicates that there's a kind of ordering to union with Christ, there's a *teleology*, at work. Those who are not united to Christ in grace are *supposed* to be. That's what they are intended to do. And there's something unfortunate about the fact that they are not; there is something very wrong about the fact that they are not, especially with those who never shall be united. The next section of my talk, where I talk about his headship over all mankind, develops this notion of potency and this idea of ordination to Christ, and give some more support for that kind of position. What's important, though, before we go on is to see that there are diverse ways in which Christ is head over all mankind; that his headship over the Church is according to the order of grace; and in some manner it extends to all mankind even in that same order.

HEADSHIP OVER ALL MANKIND

What I would like to go on to argue for, is that there is another sense of headship, where he has a natural headship over all mankind; not according to the order of grace, but according to the order of nature. Now, I have to put in here a kind of disclaimer and qualifier. First, in what I've done so far we're on firm theological ground following Thomas; the Church has defined these things, etc. Going forward I will be arguing *praeter Thomam*, beyond what Thomas says explicitly, although I think the principles of my argument are found in his works. Further, I will be going into the realm of theological opinion, and so there might be some questions about whether this is the best way to argue or whether there might be other things to consider. This is important to keep in mind. Now that being said, it's not as if we'll be departing from Church doctrine here; in fact, I will use Church doctrine to make my argument. But the case that I'm making is not something that has been defined and it's okay to not agree with me completely.

So let's talk about his headship over all mankind. We might get a hint that there's a further sense of headship that we can apply to Christ by looking a little further in the same question where we talked about Christ's headship over all mankind. That was question 8, article 3, of the *Tertia pars* of the *Summa*. If we go just a few articles down, to question 8, article 7, we find this very interesting article about the headship of Satan, or the devil, whether he can be said to be head. Thomas makes a very important distinction there. He affirms that the devil can be said to be head over hell and those who do evil in some way; but he says it's not by way of interiority: it's not an interior principle of grace by which he is head and by which they are united to him. But it's according to an external authority. And in this case the devil somehow has authority over those united to him because he's seduced them or corrupted them in some fashion and they are following in his footsteps. I'm reminded of Christ's rather harsh words to the Pharisees in the Gospel of John, where he says, "Abraham is not your father, Satan is your father"(cf. Jn 8:39–44). There is something very true about this kind of authority and headship even if it's not according to an internal principle, but rather an external principle. It seems, then, if that's true for Satan, there has to be a way in which that's true for Christ. And in fact, the Church affirms this when we celebrate the feast of Christ the King. This feast is an acknowledgement of, at the very least, Christ's external authority over all mankind and indeed all the world. And this would be enough to talk about a kind of natural headship: His authority as king comes to him by nature, by virtue of the Incarnation. So right there we could stop and say, all right, there he is, he's a natural head; because a king is, of course, a head, and Christ is head. This is fine.

But what I'm proposing to do is push this a little further. And the reason I want to push this a little further is because of something we find in the Letter to the Hebrews, in chapter 1: "But in these last days he has spoken to us by a Son, whom he appointed heir of all things, through whom also he created the world." Thomas has a very amazing question, I encourage you all to look at it: question 16 of the *Tertia pars* of the *Summa*, where he goes through all the different ways in which we can name Christ and talk about Christ, and he sorts out the heretical expressions, and the non-heretical expressions, and the expressions that aren't actually heretical but have been used danger-ously by heretics in the past, etc. And it's a very helpful question to keep these names of Christ clear so that we can speak correctly about the Incarnation. So, together with Hebrews, and as Thomas argues very clearly in that same question, we can call Christ "Creator." That is one of his names. Now we have to think about what that can possibly mean, because Christ came into the world in time and creation happened at the beginning of time. How can someone who comes posteriorly cause something that happened before him? Well, you can say, he's God, and that's true, but remember the name "Christ" names the Incarnate Word; that is, the one who came in time. But he says Christ can be called "Creator." How can this be? In order to explain this a little more clearly, and how this works, I want us to talk just briefly about the theology of the Incarnation and particularly the Hypostatic Union.

What's important is that we're talking about one hypostasis, or one supposit, with Christ, and that's why we call it the hypostatic union. There's one hypostasis but there are two natures: the divine and the human. Again, for those not familiar with scholastic terminology, nature is a term that can be confusing, because we are not talking about "Mother Nature" or something like that, or being conditioned naturally, but here it's the "what it is to be a thing," it's what makes the thing to be it. So there's a human nature and the divine nature united together in one hypostasis. This is the doctrine of the hypostatic union. But it's important to realize that, while there is this union, the two natures are not like parts. You shouldn't think of it as two parts making up a whole. Nor should you ever say that Christ is one hundred percent God and one hundred percent man. (I get what is trying to be said, and you don't have to correct people when they say that — the pious grandmother and things like that, but one hundred percent implies that you can have a different percentage, and already you're talking about parts and things like that). Rather, we say true God; true man, to indicate that there's no diminishment of the natures in the union. And that's what's important: it's true God and true man. Further, we must recall that the divine nature is not other than the person of Christ; the person is not other than the divine nature. So Christ has two natures, but it's the divine person that assumes the human nature. The Second Person assumes the human nature. And the second person is not other than the divine nature. It's not as if there was a human person there and the second person obliterated him and took his nature. It's the personhood of the one hypostasis, in virtue of the divine nature. Nevertheless, the one hypostasis is still true man. And that means he has a body, a soul, reason, will, etc. So then there are the two natures, but it's not as if they're coequal. There's no parity between the divine and human natures.

Because these natures are in one hypostasis, there are certain wonderful things that result from this. And here we come to a very important doctrine, the communication of idioms. St. Cyril of Alexandria is probably the most famous, certainly my favorite, promoter of this idea of the communication of idioms. The idea is that, because there is one hypostasis, then things undergone by the one hypostasis with two natures are said of the whole, of the hypostasis, even if the undergoing only occurs in the human nature. Okay, that's kind of abstract. What do I mean? What I mean is, we can say truly, that God was born of a virgin. How? Well in virtue of his human nature. It's not as if she was a principle of divinity from all eternity. But she is a principle of God coming into the world as man. So that's why St. Cyril argued so forcefully against Nestorius that she is truly called the Mother of God. So also we can say, on the Cross, that God died; not, of course, according to his eternal and immutable divine essence, but in his human nature. Nevertheless, this undergoing is attributed to the hypostasis, the one supposit. Now this communication of idioms can be said to work both ways, but not exactly because of what we said before, that the divine nature is there with the person, as it were: the person is the same as his nature. So it gets a little more complicated. However, because Christ is God and the name "Creator" is a name that pertains to the person, thus we can call Christ "Creator," but we don't say that it was according to his human nature that he is Creator. Rather we are saying that it is the hypostasis who is God who is the Creator. But this one hypostasis also has a human nature. So it's not according to his human nature that he is Creator, but it's according to the divine nature. Nevertheless, because of the hypostatic union (the name "Christ" implies that union), we can say that Christ is Creator.

So here is where in light of these considerations we can bring our argument together. It is in virtue of the hypostatic union that we can say that Christ is head of all mankind. And I think the best way to think about this is with a phrase I borrowed from John Saward in another context, but it applies here: Christ can be said to be head of mankind, and it's because he is God but it is as man that he is head of mankind. So he can only be head of mankind because he is God; but in order to be truly a head of mankind, it's because of his human nature. Let me explain. If he's going to be head of mankind, we have to see him as being together with mankind in some way. Well, he has the same nature as us. But he has to have order, perfection, and power. Can we say these things of Christ according to nature? Well, as is said in Hebrews 1:6 of Christ: "And again when he brings the firstborn into the world, he says, Let all God's angels worship him." In another place Paul will talk about him being the firstborn of all creation. In some way Christ is first, even in the Incarnation. He is a principle of all. As we just saw, he can be called "Creator." As quoted before: "Through whom also he created the world" (Heb 1:2). All things are created through Christ. As Creator then, and as the one through whom all things are created, he is a principle, the principle of the order. Then we have to talk about whether he can be said to have the perfection. Well, certainly. Regardless of the order of grace he is the exemplar for all mankind according to nature. And again as Hebrews says in 1:4–5, "Being so much better than the angels as he has inherited a more excellent name." So then both according to nature ,because he is God—the one hypostasis has the divine nature, but also in virtue of his perfect operations, he is said to have inherited a more excellent name. Then power. Can he be said to be head according to power? Yes. All things are in his power. As Hebrews 1:3 says, "Who being the splendor of his glory and the figure of his substance, upholding all things by the word of his power." So Christ has power over all things. Thus it is as man—because this is how he is united to all mankind, as man and together with us; but because he is God, that we are able to say that Christ is the natural head of all mankind.

A few difficulties you might wonder about: how is all mankind a body? How are we all united? This is a question.

Are we still united this way? Usually when the Fathers talk about the union of all mankind, they're talking about original sin. We're united in Adam. Thomas often talks about this and says all mankind can be called a body, and he always refers to Porphyry, where he says all men can be considered as one in some way. A difficulty with that is that Porphyry is talking about logic. It's a logical consideration. Thomas seems to take it though to have further metaphysical implications. I'm not going to get into that. But certainly, according to the authority of St. Thomas, there's a real sense in which we can all be said to be united.

Maybe another way to think about the way we are all united is in virtue of the Incarnation; perhaps due to this, there is an even greater unity to mankind; maybe mankind is a body more perfectly in virtue of the Incarnation. And what I mean by that is, when Adam fell and introduced a kind of disorder into his own members, there also seems to be a disorder in the whole of mankind as a consequence. And we don't end up being as united as we were intended to be. With Christ, however, coming into the world, since the one who is the principle of our being, the one through whom we live and move and have our being (Acts 17:28), is one of us, then perhaps mankind is now considered more united in Christ.

This is where I think I can help cast some insight on the last two senses in which Christ is said to be head over all men in the order of grace. Because if there's this union, this natural headship, you see there's a kind of natural ordination to the perfection of that union with Christ according to the order of Christ. And so the sense of *telos* is made stronger in those two ways of Christ being united to men in potency. Consequently it's in virtue of Christ as man but because he is God and what follows upon that that we can call him natural head of all mankind, both according to external authority — Christ as King — and even according to interiority, as I attempted to argue for in the last part of my talk.

9

Quæstiones Disputatæ

REV. THOMAS CREAN, O.P.
Magister Disputationis

PREFATORY NOTE

The highlight of every Summer Theology Program of the Saint Albert the Great Center for Scholastic Studies is the scholastic disputation with which it culminates. The format of the disputation is as follows. All participants in the Summer Theology Program are divided into two teams: a "St. Albert" team and a "St. Thomas" team. Three questions are posed and each team is assigned to argue either the affirmative or the negative for each question. An afternoon session and another session the following morning are dedicated to preparation of the arguments.

The teams then come together and are ranged against each other before the seat of the Magister. Six arguments affirming the first question are delivered by members of one team followed by six arguments denying the same question from the other team. A five minute recess is then given to allow each team to formulate rebuttals against the arguments put forward by the other team. With the disputation back in session, each team is allotted five minutes to deliver its rebuttals. This concludes the first question. The whole process is then repeated for the second question and again for the third.

A three hour recess is then given during which the Magister prepares his authoritative response to the three questions and his replies to the arguments and rebuttals put forward on each side. His delivery of this response concludes the scholastic disputation.

QUÆSTIO I

Incipit disputatio. Quaeritur primo utrum ille qui legis Mosaicae ritus exerceat Deum offendat. Being translated that is, whether he who performs the rites of the Old Law offends God.

ARGUMENTS OF THE PROPOSITION

PROP. 1. It would seem that he does offend God. The sinner, as such, is displeasing to God. "Thou hatest all the workers of iniquity" (Ps 5:7). "But unto God the wicked and his wickedness are hateful alike" (Wis 14:9). Hence, one who approaches the rites of the New Law in a state of sin offends God. But all who approached the rites of the Old Law were in a state of sin: "For all have sinned and fall short of the glory of God" (Rom 3:23). Therefore, in performing these rites, they offended God.

PROP. 2. Just as God punished Pharaoh for hardness of heart, so too he punished the children of Israel by imposing a law with which He was not pleased, as He says through the prophet Ezekiel: "I gave them statutes that were not good, and judgments, in which they shall not live, and I polluted them in their own gifts" (Ezek 20:25–26). Hence, St. Paul states that the giving of the Law made those who received it more conscious of their sin and therefore more culpable for it.

PROP. 3. If we refer to the period before the coming of Christ, the Lord Himself tells us what He thinks of the rites of the law, by the prophet Isaiah: "Offer sacrifice no more in vain: incense is an abomination to me. The new moons, and the sabbaths, and other festivals I will not abide, your assemblies are wicked" (Isa 1:13). All the more abominable are these rites when performed after the coming of Christ, as Paul testifies: "For as many as are of the works of the law, are under a curse" (Gal 3:10). Therefore, both before and after the coming of Christ, he who performs the rites of the Old Law offends God.

PROP. 4. Christ's death by crucifixion was an offense to God, as it was a great sin on the part of those who did it, which included both Jews and Gentiles. Now, the rites of the Old Law are a prefiguration of this sacrifice. Therefore, they too are offensive to God.

PROP. 5. After Christ's definitive sacrifice, it is clear that the rites of the Old Law are offensive to God. However, during Christ's life and before, the same rites were not efficacious. Therefore they were done in vain. But God is offended by that which is in vain, since vanity or emptiness is opposed to being, and God is being itself: "I am who am" (Ex 3:14). Therefore, performing such rites was offensive to God.

PROP. 6. God is offended when due honor is not paid to Him. However, nothing less than God can give due honor to God, for there is an infinite distance between the Creator and the creature. Hence, any rite other than that of Christ is offensive to Him. Therefore, all the rites of the Old Law are offensive.

ARGUMENTS OF THE OPPOSITION

OPP. 1. Under the Old Law God established the rite known as *Pascha* (or the Pasch) and commanded us to keep it forever. For in the book of Exodus 12:14, he says: "And this day shall be a memorial to you, and you shall keep it a feast to the Lord in your generations with an everlasting observance (*sempiternam*). Again, in verse 17 of the same chapter, God said: "And you shall observe the feast of Unleavened Bread, for in the same day I will bring forth your army out of the land of Egypt, and you shall keep this day in your generations by a perpetual observance (*ritu perpetuum*). Again, in verse 24 God said: "Thou shalt keep this thing as a law for thee and thy children forever (*usque in aeternam*). Now God has told us that keeping the Eucharist is keeping the Pasch. For it is written in the First Letter of St. Paul to the Corinthians 5:7 that: "For Christ our Pasch is sacrificed (*etenim*

Pascha nostrum immolatus est Christus). And God does not lie, as he said in Numbers 23:19, "God is not a man, that he should lie, nor is he a son of man, that he should be changed. Hath he said then, and will not do? Hath he spoken, and will not fulfill?" Therefore, he who celebrates the Eucharist observes a rite of the Old Law, keeps the commandment, pleases God, and does not offend him.

OPP. 2. The phrase "offends God" indicates sin. The Angelic Doctor cites the Damascene and the Philosopher to say that what is done through ignorance is involuntary. For sin to occur one must have grave matter, full knowledge, and full consent of the will. Therefore, a Jew inculpably ignorant of the New Law cannot offend God by performing the rites of the Old Law.

OPP. 3. If the Church were to approve the rites of the Old Law, they could not offend God. Benedict XIV approved the rites of the Old Law in *Ex quo*: "The Church of Christ has the power to renew the obligation to observe some of the old precepts for just and serious reasons despite their abrogation by the New Law. However, the precepts whose main function was to foreshadow the coming of the Messiah should not be restored." Many of the rites of the Old Law do not foreshadow the coming of the Messiah and are observed by the Church, such as the churching of women. Therefore, he who performs these rites of the Old Law does not offend God.

OPP. 4. According to the Council of Florence, the legal prescriptions of the Old Testament could be retained from the time of Christ's passion until the promulgation of the Gospel. But today there remain people who have not heard the Gospel. It follows, therefore, that the Gospel has not yet been promulgated. Therefore, he who performs the rites of the Old Law does not offend God since we are not in the time following the promulgation of the Gospel.

OPP. 5. The natural law requires one to worship God by sacrifice. But the Old Law also prescribes sacrifice. Therefore, since it is in accord with the natural law to offer

sacrifice, he who is aware of the Old Law and is in ignorance of the New Law, would sin by not offering sacrifice.

OPP. 6. He who educates others for the sake of giving
sound catechesis about the Passion of our Lord and the
Holy Sacrifice of the Mass is very pleasing to God. But
the rites of the Old Law pertaining to the Seder meal,
when they are celebrated as a "Passover-style-dinner,"
"educates others for the sake of giving sound catechesis
about the Passion of our Lord and the Holy Sacrifice of
the Mass," as argued by Dr. Peter Kwasniewski.[1]

Therefore, he who celebrates the rites of the Old Law
not only does not offend God, but is rather very pleasing
to God. Proof of the first premise: It is pleasing to God to
do the will of the Father. But the will of the Father is that
his Son should suffer and die on Calvary for our redemption, and that we should participate in that sacrifice on
Calvary through faith in the sacraments. But faith in the
sacraments is only built and fortified through education
and catechesis of the sacramental symbolism. Proof of the
second premise: The rites of the Old Law all prefigure
Christ's passion and the Eucharist. Thus if the rites of the
Seder meal are celebrated as pointing to the Passion that
has already occurred and to the Eucharist present among
us, then they serve to educate about the passion and the
Eucharist. Therefore, he who celebrates the rites of the
Old Law not only does not offend God, but is rather very
pleasing to God. Proof of the first premise: It is pleasing
to God to do the will of the Father. But the will of the
Father is that his Son should suffer and die on Calvary for
our redemption, and that we should participate in that
sacrifice on Calvary through faith in the sacraments. But
faith in the sacraments is only built and fortified through
education and catechesis of the sacramental symbolism.
Proof of the second premise: The rites of the Old Law all

---

[1] See "Should Christians Celebrate a 'Seder Meal'?," *New Liturgical Movement*, February 22, 2016, https://www.newliturgicalmovement. org/2016/02/should-christians-celebrate-seder-meal.html.

prefigure Christ's passion and the Eucharist. Thus if the
rites of the Seder meal are celebrated as pointing to the
Passion that has already occurred and to the Eucharist
present among us, then they serve to educate about the
passion and the Eucharist.

RESPONSE OF THE MAGISTER

Let me first of all say how impressed I was by the
standard of the arguments put forward this morning, at
least in most cases. And I will try to answer everything
that was said, but given the number of points that were
made, I may well miss something out, so please excuse
me if I do, and feel free to raise it later in the day. So
the first question was, "Whether he who performs the
rites of the Old Law offends God?"

I answer that, as St. Thomas says, "The rites of the Old
Law were directed toward the worship of God." And as
he also says, "External worship should correspond to
the internal worship by which we honor God in faith,
hope, and charity." Now, although the faith and hope
of Christians are in substance the same as the faith and
hope of the Jews under the Old Law, nevertheless they
differ in state. Under the Old Law, faith and hope were
placed in the Redeemer who was to come and in heavenly blessings to which he would grant the people access
when he came. Under the New Law, our faith and hope
are placed in the Redeemer who has already come and
in the heavenly goods which he has now made available
to us. As the Apostle says in Hebrews 10, "We have confidence to enter the sanctuary by the blood of Jesus, by
the new and living way which he opened for us through
the veil, that is, through his flesh." Therefore, just as we
must avoid offending God by saying the words, "that the
Redeemer has not yet come" or "that heaven is closed to
mankind," so we must also avoid professing such false-
hoods by our deeds. And hence, since the ceremonies
of the Old Law were instituted to signify the Savior still

to come, according to the words of St. Paul, "the Law having a shadow of the good things to come," we must not conform ourselves to the ceremonies of the Old Law by following the instructions which Moses gave to the people of Israel in these matters. And Moses himself foreshadowed the abrogation of his own law by breaking the tablets of stone, which he had received from God, at the foot of Mount Sinai, as related in Exodus 32:19.

Moreover, this teaching is confirmed by the authority of the Church. The Ecumenical Council of Florence, in its Decree for the Copts *Cantate Domino*, promulgated in 1442, declares as follows: "The Sacrosanct Roman Church, founded by the voice of our Lord and Savior, firmly believes, professes, and teaches that the legal things of the Old Testament, that is, of the Mosaic Law, which are divided into ceremonies, holy sacrifices, and sacraments, because they are established to signify something in the future, although they were suited to the divine worship at that time, after our Lord's coming, which had been signified by them, ceased, and the sacraments of the New Law began." And it continues: "Whoever after the passion still placed hope in these matters of the Law and submitted himself to them as necessary for salvation, as if faith in Christ could not save without them, sinned mortally." Yet it goes on: "It [the Roman Church] does not deny that after the passion of Christ, up to the promulgation of the Gospel, they could have been observed so long as they were believed to be in no way necessary for salvation. But it [the Church] asserts that after the promulgation of the Gospel they cannot be observed without the loss of eternal salvation. All therefore who after that time observed circumcision and the Sabbath and the other requirements of the law, it declares alien to the Christian faith and not in the least bit to participate in eternal salvation." Pius XII, in his encyclical *Mystici Corporis*, summarized all this teaching briefly by saying, "On the Cross the Old Law died, soon to be buried and to be a bearer of death." It follows, then, that the Old Law cannot properly speaking be observed without denying the coming of Christ, thereby offering an affront to God who did not spare his own Son, but delivered him up for our sake.

REPLIES TO THE ARGUMENTS OF THE PROPOSITION

So now to reply to the arguments. And first, then, I shall reply to the arguments in favor of the thesis, that say that he who performs the rites of the Old Law offends God.

AD PROP. 1. To the first one, that whoever approaches the rites of the Old Law in the Old Testament did so in a state of sin, and thereby offended God, I answer that, as was said in one of the rebuttals, it was not necessary that all did approach the rites of the Old Law in a state of sin in the Old Testament even though the rites themselves did not grant sanctifying grace.

AD PROP. 2–3. Arguments two and three likewise argued *a fortiori*, that is to say, they argued that already in the Old Testament the rites of the Old Law were displeasing to God, therefore much more so in the New. However, the speakers did not explain, I think, the reason for the *a fortiori*, and nor, I think, did they establish that the rites did displease God before the New Testament. When Ezekiel 20 says that the Law was not good, it meant that it could not justify those who observed it, not that it was an offense to observe it in those days. Again, the fact that the giving of the Law increases concupiscence, by telling us what it is that God does not want us to do, and thereby making us more interested in doing it; again, this does not prove that it was displeasing to God to obey the Old Law—just that the giving of the Law made it more difficult to observe certain precepts of the natural law. The words of Isaiah, "that incense be offered in vain"—I agree with one of the rebuttals—this means that such external sacrifices are vain if they are separated from the worship of the heart.

AD PROP. 4. To the argument that the Old Testament prefigured the crucifixion, which was a great offense to God, I answer that it prefigured the crucifixion in the way that we represent it at Mass: not insofar as it was an act of violence perpetrated by unbelievers, but insofar as it was an act of love and obedience offered by the Son.

AD PROP. 5. To the argument that the rites of the Old Law were displeasing because they were inefficacious and therefore vain and empty, and God is being and therefore dislikes anything that is not being, I reply that this argument, though ingenious, is not conclusive, because the rites of the Old Law were not entirely inefficacious, for although they did not bestow holiness they did keep alive the hope of a Redeemer.

AD PROP. 6. Finally, to the argument that the rites were displeasing because only God can pay to himself due honor, I reply that, though that is true, God is not displeased by being paid less than due honor, provided that the one who pays it does not claim to be giving God all that is due to him. In the same way our parents are not displeased by our acts of filial piety towards them, even though we can never repay them the whole debt of our existence.

REPLIES TO THE ARGUMENTS OF THE OPPOSITION

We come now to the arguments that it is pleasing to God, or at least denying that it is displeasing to God, to observe the Old Law.

AD OPP. 1. The first one observed that the Jews were taught to keep the Pasch as a perpetual observance. And also that the Pasch remains, since St. Paul says in 1 Corinthians that, "Christ our Pasch has been sacrificed"—a reference to the Holy Eucharist. I reply that this argument seems to contain its own refutation. For the Passover is commanded to the Jews to be kept forever not in itself but in its antitype that realizes it, that is to say, in the Holy Eucharist, which remains to the end of time. And in this Holy Eucharist, of course, it is not the rites of the Passover that are being observed.

AD OPP. 2. The second argument that the rites do not displease God was from the fact that a Jew today may perform them in ignorance, and that this ignorance will, or at least may, be inculpable, therefore excusing him from guilt. I answer that, although such ignorance may preserve him from punishment for his deed, the act nevertheless is in itself displeasing to God. It is rather as if someone were reading words from a book in a language that he didn't understand, and those words were understood by his hearers and were a series of insults offered to them. The person is indeed offending them and yet it is possible that he is guiltless.

AD OPP. 3. The third argument was that, according to Benedict XIV, in the letter *Ex quo*, the Church can approve some rites of the Old Law and indeed has done so, for example, in the case of the churching of women, which is taken to continue the rite of purification of women. I answer that, in this particular case, the ceremony is in fact different, since it is not purification but thanksgiving for the birth of the child which is in question and the rite of the Church refers to Christ explicitly. Nevertheless it is possible that the Church could command us to perform some rite which as a matter of fact is contained in the Law of Moses, for example, to abstain from shellfish as a matter of penance; however, if the Church did so, those who obeyed this rule would not be conforming themselves to the dictates of Moses, as they would not be abstaining from shellfish because Moses had said so but because the Church had laid it down.

AD OPP. 4. The fourth argument was that the Council of Florence says that before the promulgation of the Gospel was complete the rites of the Old Law may be observed provided one does not put one's faith in them as salvific. And the assertion was made that the promulgation of the Gospel has not yet been completed as there are still people who have not yet heard it. I answer that this is a frivolous argument because on such an argument the promulgation of the Gospel would never be finished since children will be born in each generation, by definition, until the end of the world. As the Apostles were the ones who promulgated the New Law, I say that the promulgation of the New Law must have been completed with the death of the last of the Apostles.

AD OPP. 5. The fifth argument was that natural law requires sacrifice, and that therefore whoever knows about the Old Law and not about the New, must sacrifice according to the Old Law if he is to avoid sin. I answer that it would not follow, even according to his own conscience, that he must do so unless he also erroneously believed himself to be bound by the Old Law—not just that he knew of its existence. If he did believe himself to be bound by the Old Law, then he would err, and the answer is the same as the answer given to the second argument.

AD OPP. 6. The sixth argument is that the rites of the Old Law may be observed when they are done with a good catechetical purpose, such as a Passover meal that is celebrated in order to educate us about the practices of the Jews at the time of Christ, and indeed about the nature of the Last Supper. I answer that a good intention cannot justify an action if the immediate object of the action is intrinsically disordered. So just as we would not please God by crucifying an innocent person even if our aim was simply to show forth the sufferings that Christ endured, so also we would not please him by conforming ourselves to the rites by which Moses taught the people that the Savior had not yet come.

REPLIES TO THE REBUTTALS

I come now to the mutual refutations. In fact, most of them, I think, have already been dealt with in the answers I have already given. A couple of points have not yet been dealt with.

AD REB. 1. Someone argued that it would be all right to observe those ceremonies of the Old Law, those observances of the Old Law, that do not signify the passion of Christ—for example, abstaining from pork or shellfish. I answer that if these practices were done because Moses had commanded them, and not simply from a personal preference such as dislike for shellfish, then they would be a way of conforming oneself to the Old Testament faith, since all these ceremonies were designed to prepare the Jews to receive the Messiah by marking them out as a people distinct from all the other peoples of the earth. Therefore it would still be illegitimate to observe these ceremonies on the grounds that Moses had commanded them.

AD REB. 2. Someone put forward the argument that the sacrifice of Abel pleased God, but that was not a rite of the Old Law, so it is outside our question.

AD REB. 3. Finally, someone suggested that a Passover meal celebrated by Christians could be a form of play-acting and not a form of observing the Old Law. I answer that, as with the suggestion that it could be a form of catechesis, this still concerns the final intention of those who are involved, the intention here being not catechesis but diverting themselves, whereas the immediate object of the act would still, in my judgment, be disordered.

QUÆSTIO II

Quaeritur secundo utrum sanguinis effusio necesse sit ad peccata remittenda. Being translated that is, whether the shedding of blood is necessary for the remission of sins.

ARGUMENTS OF THE PROPOSITION

PROP. 1. As St. John says, "As Moses lifted up the serpent in the desert, so must the Son of Man be lifted up, that whosoever believes in him may not perish but may have life everlasting" (Jn 3:14). But this lifting up is the crucifixion, and crucifixion necessitates the shedding of blood. Therefore, the shedding of blood is necessary for the remission of sins. To perish, that is, to die, is the consequence of sin. And in order to remove the effect, we must remove the cause. So, when St. John says, "So must the Son of Man be lifted up, that whosoever believes in him may have life everlasting," it means that the shedding of blood is necessary for the remission of sins.

PROP. 2. In the book of Genesis, Adam and Eve's shame of their nakedness is indicative of their sinfulness. Adam and Eve attempted to remedy their shame by making clothing out of fig leaves. This is ineffective. So God makes clothing for both of them from animal skins, taking away their shame by the slaughter of animals. Therefore, the shedding of blood is necessary for the remission of sins.

PROP. 3. On the question of whether the shedding of blood is necessary for the remission of sins, we would do well to take into account the sacrifices of Cain and Abel. For, as stated in Hebrews 11:4, "By faith Abel offered to God a sacrifice exceeding that of Cain, by which he obtained a testimony that he was just, God giving testimony to his gifts." But Cain made his offering from the fruits of the earth, which we know was not pleasing to God. And Abel made an offering of the firstlings of his flock. Thus Aquinas states that Abel's sacrifice exceeds that of Cain "not in quantity but in preciousness." And Matthew describes Abel as just, meaning that he did not have sin. Therefore, his sacrifice remitted his sin, and thus blood sacrifice alone is acceptable to God.

PROP. 4. By sinning we destroy the life of God in us insofar as we deprive ourselves of sanctifying grace. But justice demands that we repay to God in like manner for having destroyed his supernatural life of grace which he gave to us. But, after the loss of the supernatural life of grace, the only life that remains to us is our life according to nature. Therefore, in order to repay God for having destroyed his supernatural life of grace, we must give him in turn our natural life. But the natural life of man is in his blood. For, as it says in Leviticus 17:14, "The life of all flesh is in the blood," for the blood is that by which we live. Therefore, in order to repay for sins, one must give one's blood to God as a payment for having destroyed the life of grace. But one cannot give one's blood to another without it first being shed. Therefore, the shedding of blood is necessary for the remission of sins.

PROP. 5. Our Lord has told us in the Gospel of Luke 24:26 that it was necessary that Christ suffer in order to enter into his glory. The suffering of Christ, as told to us by the prophets, is his death for the transgressions of sinners, which involves the spilling of blood. Entering into his glory involves, by virtue of the Gospel of John 17:9–10, that those Christ has called to enter into the kingdom with his Father are saved and their sins remitted. Therefore, because the suffering is equal to the spilling of his blood and the glory equal to the resurrection of the dead and the remission of sins, it is necessary for the spilling of Christ's blood to happen in order for sins to be remitted on behalf of us.

PROP. 6. In John 6:53–54 Jesus says, "Unless you eat the flesh and drink the blood of the Son of Man you have no life in you. Whoever eats my flesh and drinks my blood has eternal life and I will raise him up at the last day." One cannot have eternal life without the remission of sins and one cannot drink someone's blood unless it has first been shed. Therefore, there must be shedding of blood in order for us to drink Christ's blood, which is necessary for the remission of sins.

ARGUMENTS OF THE OPPOSITION

OPP. 1. In the Old Testament, God at times forgives sins without the shedding of blood. In Proverbs 16:6 we read, "By faithfulness, iniquity is atoned for." And 2 Chronicles 30 recounts how Hezekiah's prayer for the forgiveness of the people was heard. In the New Testament, the Lord frequently forgives the sins of those who come to him, such as the woman caught in adultery (Jn 8), or the woman who washes his feet with her tears (Lk 7), on account of their faith, without the shedding of blood. Therefore, the shedding of blood is not always necessary for the remission of sins.

OPP. 2. Everything said in the Old Testament was said in figure. Now blood represents life (cf. Lev 17:11). Therefore what is actually necessary for the forgiveness of sins is not blood, but the reality it signifies, namely, the rededication of one's life to God. "It is the spirit that gives life, the flesh is of no avail" (Jn 6:63), and "I desired mercy, and not sacrifice, and the knowledge of God more than holocausts" (Hos 6:6).

OPP. 3. If the shedding of blood were necessary, then Our Lord's shedding of blood, by which the sins of the world are forgiven, would have been necessary. However, Christ, as God, is all-powerful and supremely free; therefore His shedding of blood was a gift and a sign of superabundant love. Now the *ratio* of gift and the *ratio* of necessity are opposed to each other. Therefore his shedding of blood was a gift and a sign of superabundant love, not a matter of necessity.

OPP. 4. The Holy Mass is a propitiatory sacrifice by which sins are forgiven. But Holy Mass is an unbloody sacrifice, as the Council of Trent teaches. Therefore, for the remission of sins, there is no need for the shedding of blood.

OPP. 5. Every time someone sincerely receives the sacraments of baptism, penance, or extreme unction, sins are remitted. Now, in none of these sacraments is there the shedding of blood. "A sacrifice to God is an afflicted spirit; a humble and contrite heart, O God, you will not spurn" (Ps 50:19). Therefore, for the remission of sins, there is no need for the shedding of blood.

OPP. 6. There are three kinds of necessity: absolute necessity, hypothetical necessity, and the necessity of fittingness. The only thing that is absolutely necessary is

God. Moreover, if the shedding of blood were necessary hypothetically, it must be that a creature could not be forgiven without it. But God in His freedom can remit any sin at any time, and to say the contrary is to impugn divine freedom. Nor could it be necessary according to fittingness. For it is men who are placated by the shedding of blood: "An eye for an eye, a tooth for a tooth, a hand for a hand, a foot for a foot," as it is written in Ex 21:24, whereas we read of God: "as the heavens are exalted above the earth, so are my ways exalted above your ways, and my thoughts above your thoughts" (Is 55:9). It is therefore unfitting to say that God requires blood in exchange for wrongdoing. Therefore the shedding of blood is not necessary in any way for the remission of sins.

RESPONSE OF THE MAGISTER

I answer that a thing may be said to be necessary for the attaining of some end in two senses: first, if the end cannot be attained without it, as some vehicle is necessary in order to cross the ocean; secondly, if the end is attained in a better and more fitting way with it, as some vehicle is necessary to travel from Norcia to Rome.

In the first way the shedding of blood is not necessary for the remission of sins, since God could have accepted some suffering of Christ which fell short of the shedding of blood as nevertheless a full and abundant satisfaction for our sins, or he could, without derogating from his own justice, have forgiven the sins of men without full satisfaction, maybe just in response to man's own prayer or feelings of contrition, or even without these, just as a householder may, without any injustice, forgive a poor man who has stolen some of his property and cannot afford to make restitution.

Nevertheless, in the second sense the shedding of blood is necessary for the remission of each and every sin, since this end of remission is best and most fittingly attained by this means. For sin is a turning towards a creature away from God who gives life to all living things, and principally who gives life to the human soul, which he vivifies by his grace. Hence our Lord says, "I am the way and the truth and the life." The sinner therefore is one who prefers to live by means of some creature rather than by God. It is therefore fitting that in order to be reconciled to God he show himself willing to do without the life of some creature that is dear to him in order to live by his Creator, as King Hezekiah said in his sickness, in Isaiah 38, "O Lord, if the life of my spirit be in such things as these, Thou shalt correct me and make me live." Now, according to Leviticus 17, "the life of the flesh is in the blood." Therefore, in order that the death of some created life may be both brought about and plainly signified, so that the sinner may be reconciled to God, it is necessary that there be an effusion of blood.

For this reason, God ordained that the redemption of the world should be brought about by the passion of Christ and the shedding of his precious blood, and that this one sufficient sacrifice should be foreshadowed by the bloody sacrifices of the Old Testament, from the sacrifice of Abel the just up to the lamb slain in the Temple on the morning of Good Friday. Furthermore, blood, along with water, flowed from our Lord's side after his sufferings were already completed in order to show that our sins would continue to be forgiven in the Church through a new and mystical shedding of his blood. Hence it is written in Hebrews 10, that the Law had but "a shadow of the good things to come," that is, of the body and blood of Christ, whereas we have the true form of these realities.

REPLIES TO THE ARGUMENTS OF THE PROPOSITION

I turn now to the arguments put forward on both sides of this question. First of all the arguments defending the thesis that the shedding of blood is necessary for remission:

AD PROP. 1. The first one was a quotation from St. John's Gospel, "as Moses lifted up the serpent in the desert so must the Son of Man must be lifted up, so that all who believe in him may have eternal life." And eternal life is only possible through the remission of sins and the lifting up of the Son of Man, which is the crucifixion. Therefore, the crucifixion is said to be necessary for the remission of sins. I agree with this provided that one considers this to be not an absolute necessity, but as I said at the beginning, a hypothetical necessity, that is to say, given God's decision to bring our salvation about in this supremely fitting way.

AD PROP. 2. The second argument was that Adam and Eve's shame, symbolizing their sin, was remedied by skins which were obtained from the killing of animals, and this is a shedding of blood. I agree with this argument provided that one realizes that the shedding of the blood of the animals, in this case for Adam and Eve, had no power in itself to take away sins but was simply a symbol that Christ's precious blood would be shed for us and it was his merits that were applied to Adam and Eve when they repented.

AD PROP. 3. The third argument was that Cain and Abel offered different sacrifices and that Cain's was unacceptable because it was from vegetables and that Abel's was acceptable because it involved the first of his flock. I agree that this is a good argument, again provided we remember that Abel's sacrifice was not intrinsically efficacious, but only pleasing because it represented his faith in the lamb slain from the foundation of the world in God's foreknowledge.

AD PROP. 4. Number four was that we destroy God's life in us by sin, and therefore to have the overcoming of sin — reconciliation with God — there must be a repayment made of some life, which is by a shedding of blood, according to Leviticus 17. I agree that this is a fitting argument, as I also mentioned in the corpus of my reply.

AD PROP. 5. The fifth argument was that Luke 24 says it was necessary that Christ should suffer, thus fulfilling the prophets and so enter into his glory, and that the prophets foretold the crucifixion, and that Christ's glory includes the glorification of the mystical body who enter the resurrection to life by virtue of his precious blood. And I agree with this argument and praise it for its originality and profundity.

AD PROP. 6. The sixth argument was that John 6 says that unless we drink the blood of the Son of Man and eat his flesh we have no life in us, and that blood cannot be drunk unless it has been shed. I agree that this is a reference to the fact that the shedding of blood is necessary for the remission of sins, but I note that it is not by reason of a shedding in the normal sense of the word that we can receive it in Holy Communion.

REPLIES TO THE ARGUMENTS OF THE OPPOSITION

So now the arguments in favor of remission without the shedding of blood.

AD OPP. 1. The first refers to various passages in the Old and New Testament that speak of forgiveness of sins without mentioning the shedding of blood, such as Proverbs 16 and 2 Chronicles. I answer that the faith by which these people obtained the forgiveness of their sins was faith in the Savior who would come and shed his blood for us, so the remission was not obtained independently of all shedding of blood. And I note also that in the Old Testament such faith would have to have been accompanied by sin offerings in the Temple, where animals were slain, just as in the New Testament such faith would have to be accompanied by assistance at Holy Mass.

AD OPP. 2. The second argument was that blood is only ever a figure of what is truly important, namely our rededication of ourselves to God after sin, and therefore blood is not necessary. I answer that this argument shows that the blood alone, considered as a physical substance, is not what reconciles us to God, but it does not show that the remission is obtained without it. It does not show that the blood is not a *necessary condition* for the remission of sins. The obedience and love of Christ that saved us, and the obedience and love by which we unite ourselves to him, went as far as his shedding of blood on the Cross. So the shedding of blood, not considered in abstraction but in the spiritual dispositions of our Lord, *did* save us — not considered as physical substance, but considered as a means of expressing the obedience and love for God.

AD OPP. 3. The third argument was that the notions of gift and necessity are contrary. Therefore, since Christ's life was a gift of himself to God, it could not have been a necessity. I answer that it was not necessary for God to send us a gift at all and that suffices to resolve the apparent contradiction. But given his will to save us in this way, it became therefore necessary for Christ to give himself freely for us, as the only way in which God's decree could be fulfilled. In other words, God willed by a hypothetical necessity that we should be saved by a free act of Christ, and that implies no contradiction.

AD OPP. 4. The fourth argument, presented to us in the language of the Church, was that the Council of Trent defined that the Mass is an unbloody sacrifice and nevertheless it remits our sins. I answer that this is very true, and that God willed that the Mass should be a sacrifice by the mystical separation of our Lord's body and blood, which is the most perfect possible representation of the physical shedding of the blood upon the Cross. And therefore the Mass does not obtain forgiveness for us independently of the blood that was shed upon the Cross. For it is a sacrifice precisely insofar as it represents that shedding. Furthermore, the Mass also applies to us the merits and satisfactions of Christ which he won for us upon the Cross.

AD OPP. 5. In a somewhat similar way, to the fifth argument that baptism and other sacraments gain the remission of our sins, I reply that they do so, but not independently of the Cross, for they apply to us the merits and graces that Christ acquired for us upon the Cross. Again, it is the continuous offering of the holy sacrifice of the Mass, representing, as I said in considering the previous objection, the bloody sacrifice of the Cross, which gains for Christians and unbelievers the actual graces necessary to receive the sacraments in a fruitful way. Therefore, these sacraments are not received independently of the shedding of blood.

AD OPP. 6. The sixth argument was that it is man and not God who requires an eye for an eye, a tooth for a tooth, a hand for a hand, a foot for a foot. I answer that man participates imperfectly in the justice of God, and therefore he is capable of enacting punishments that will help to restore the balance in society. He is not, however, able by such punishments to take away the guilt of the offender. This can only be done by God infusing grace into our souls. But as I have already argued, this is done not independently of the shedding of Christ's blood.

REPLIES TO THE REBUTTALS

I come to any remaining arguments that were put forward in the mutual rebuttals.

AD REB. 1. One suggestion was that the argument that Adam and Eve were clothed with skins from slaughtered animals and that this foreshadows the shedding of blood, does not hold water, because these skins could have been made by God *ex nihilo*. I answer that I suppose they could have been. But nevertheless the common consent of theologians is that after the six days of work described in Genesis 1, only human souls are created *ex nihilo*. And it also seems contrary to the wisdom of God to do something by special act of creation which could be done using things which are already in creation.

AD REB. 2. The second point to cover is that, on this same question, it was argued that the covering up of Adam and Eve simply covered up their nakedness, and therefore has nothing to do with the remission of sin. I answer that the nakedness of Adam and Eve, for which they felt shame in God's presence — hence Adam hid himself, because he was naked, from the sight of God — that this nakedness is a cause of shame before God. And therefore that which hides our shame is fittingly seen to be a symbol of God's remission, since it is only by the remission of sins that our shame can be really hidden from God's sight, so that he no longer sees anything in us of which we need be ashamed.

AD REB. 3. The next point that came up was that, far from Cain being rejected because he only offered vegetables, he would have been very pleasing to God had he offered vegetables and also had charity. I answer that it seems to me that if Cain had had charity and therefore also faith, he would have been moved to have offered an animal. However, I cannot avail myself of the argument that was put against this by the other side, that it would be Molinist to say what God would have done in hypothetical circumstances, because a sixteenth century pope forbade the Dominicans from calling Molinists heretics.

AD REB. 4. It was argued also that it was repugnant to think that God could be appeased by blood. I answer that it would certainly be repugnant to reason to think that God could be appeased by blood insofar as it is a material substance or pain in itself; but not that it is repugnant to think that he could be appeased in this way insofar as these things are the necessary concomitants of a supreme act of charity and obedience.

AD REB. 5. It was argued that the shedding of blood is necessary because it is not enough simply for us to offer ourselves — rededicate ourselves — to God because there is nothing in the intellect which is not first in the senses. But this argument does not seem to me to follow since speech is something that is in the senses. And so this does not prove that we could not be saved by simply being told to rededicate ourselves to God, without the shedding of blood.

QUÆSTIO III

Quaeritur tertio utrum sufficiat, ut Deo placabilis quis efficiatur, quod credat ille Deum esse necnon remuneratorem exstare inquirentibus se. Being translated that is, whether to please God it is sufficient to believe that he is and is a rewarder of those who seek him.

ARGUMENTS OF THE PROPOSITION

PROP. 1. It would seem that it is sufficient. For in the existence of God are contained all divine perfections, and his providence comprises all effects towards creatures. Therefore, one who believes in his existence and providence virtually believes all that can be believed. And therefore it is sufficient.

PROP. 2. Original sin was caused by Adam and Eve's seeking of the knowledge of good and evil instead of observing God's commandment not to eat the fruit of the tree. The purpose of their eating of the fruit was to be as gods. To seek to be as gods, however, is to doubt that God is a rewarder of those who seek him. Now doubting is opposed to believing. If, therefore, Adam and Eve had not sought to be as gods, they and their descendants would have been in a state of original grace and therefore pleasing to God, simply in virtue of believing that he exists and is a rewarder of those who seek him.

PROP. 3. If it were not sufficient, we would not be offered as examples saints of the Old Testament — for example, Abel, Noah, and Joshua — of whom it is not narrated that they believed in more than God's existence and providence, for then God would seem to be lying to us, giving examples we should not imitate. Moreover, if this faith was sufficient for them, it should also be sufficient for us, since we are told: "God is not a man, that he should lie, nor as the son of man, that he should be changed" (Num 23:19).

PROP. 4. It is possible for men to know by natural reason that God is and is a rewarder of those who seek Him. And it pleases God to be known in this way by men, for Job, who was a Gentile, nevertheless knew God and pleased him. However, belief, because it does not see, requires more trust and is therefore more pleasing to God. Therefore, to please God it is more than sufficient to believe that God is and is a rewarder of those who seek him.

PROP. 5. St. Paul holds against the Gentiles only that they failed to acknowledge God and his attributes: "Because that which is known of God is manifest in them. For God hath manifested it unto them. For the invisible things of him, from the creation of the world, are clearly seen, being understood by the things that are made; his eternal power also, and divinity: so that they are inexcusable" (Rom 1:19–20). Thus he gives the same teaching as he does in the Epistle to the Hebrews. But if more had been required for salvation, he would not have failed to make it known. Therefore it is sufficient to believe that God is and is a rewarder of those who seek him.

PROP. 6. The Second Vatican Ecumenical Council states in the dogmatic constitution on the Church *Lumen Gentium*: "The plan of salvation also includes those who acknowledge the Creator" (n. 16). Therefore, it would seem that it is sufficient for the salvation of at least certain individuals that they acknowledge the Creator, that is, the existence of the one true God and his governance over creation.

ARGUMENTS OF THE OPPOSITION

OPP. 1. The Sacred and Ecumenical Council of Florence solemnly defines that, "not only pagans but also Jews or heretics and schismatics, cannot share in eternal life and will go into the everlasting fire which was prepared for the devil and his angels, unless they are joined to the Catholic Church before the end of their lives." But Jews, heretics and schismatics as well as some pagans believe in God and in his providence. Therefore, belief in God and his providence is only necessary and not sufficient to please God.

OPP. 2. The Sacred and Ecumenical Council of Florence also solemnly defines, "Whosoever would be saved before all else he must profess the Catholic Faith, which faith unless he profess whole and entire with all its parts he will most certainly perish everlastingly. And the Catholic Faith is this, that we worship the one God in Trinity and the Trinity in Unity neither dividing the substance nor confusing the persons." Therefore, belief in God and his providence is only necessary and not sufficient to please God.

OPP. 3. St. Peter says of the Holy Name of Jesus that there is no other name under heaven given to men by which we may be saved (Acts 4:12). Thus the Catechism of the Catholic Church teaches, quoting the very words of the Epistle to the Hebrews, "Believing in Jesus and in the one who sent Him for our Salvation is necessary to receive that salvation. For 'without faith it is impossible to please God' or enter into the fellowship of His sons. For without faith no one has ever been justified nor shall anyone be saved but he who perseveres until the end" (CCC 161). Therefore, belief in God and his providence is only necessary and not sufficient to please God.

OPP. 4. The Holy Office under Pope Clement XI in 1703 decreed that a missionary may not baptize a perilously ill pagan who knows nothing of Christian truth but knows only "of God and some of his attributes, especially his justice in rewarding and punishing." The Holy Office responds: "A missionary should not baptize one who does not believe explicitly in the Lord Jesus Christ, but is bound to instruct him about all those matters which are necessary by a necessity of means [expressly the Trinity and the Incarnation]." Therefore, belief in God and his providence is only necessary and not sufficient to please God.

OPP. 5. The existence of God and his providence may be known with certainty by reason; therefore, if assent to these things were sufficient to please God, it would be possible to achieve this by human effort unaided by

revelation and grace. But this is not the Gospel of grace
but the pride of Satan who said, "I will make myself like
the Most High." Therefore, belief in God and his providence is only necessary and not sufficient to please God.

OPP. 6. The Gospel by which we are saved is Good
News. It is good because its reception by those to whom
it is proclaimed accomplishes their salvation. It is news
because the truths it contains cannot be known by reason
alone. But God's existence and providence can be known
by reason alone. If these alone sufficed for salvation then
the Gospel would not be news. Furthermore, the other
truths of the Gospel would be not a proclamation of
grace but the imposition of a burdensome precept and
so, like the Pharisees, the Apostles would "cross land and
sea to make a single proselyte and yet make him twice
as much a child of hell as themselves" (cf. Mt 23:15). But
on the contrary the prophet says, "How beautiful on the
mountains are the feet of him who brings good news"
(Is 52:7). Therefore, belief in God and his providence is
only necessary and not sufficient to please God.

RESPONSE OF THE MAGISTER

I answer that, according to the teaching of the Apostle, in
Hebrews 11:6, faith is necessary to please God because faith
is the means by which we come to him. Therefore, in order
to know which truths of faith it is necessary to believe in
order to please him, we must consider how faith enables us
to draw near to him. Now that which principally separates
a man from God is sin. Therefore, in order to have the
kind of faith that will enable us to draw near to God and
therefore to please him, we must have faith in those truths
that pertain to our deliverance from sin. Jesus Christ is for
all mankind the one who delivers them from sin. Hence we
read in 1 John, "He is the propitiation for our sins, and not
for ours only, but for those of the whole world." Therefore,
ever since sin entered the world through the deception
of the devil, it has been necessary for all who wish to be

delivered from their sins and to come to God, to believe in the only Son of God as their Savior.

However, this belief in the Son of God as Savior has been able to take different forms before and after Christ actually saved us by dying for us on the Cross. After the fall of man, but before our Lord died for us, it was possible to please God, providing of course that one's works corresponded to one's faith, by believing simply in the Redeemer whom God would send, or even in the salvation that God would give. Thus many even of the Jews lacked a clear belief in the future Incarnation of the Word. It was possible at that time to be justified by believing simply and without further specification in the Savior or salvation that God would grant us, because at that time this act of belief contained implicitly, but actually, Jesus Christ as its object. For God knew that the Savior he would grant would be his Son, and the people in believing in the Savior whom God would send, meant the Savior whom God now knows that he will send, and therefore they believed actually, though implicitly, in Christ.

Once our Lord had suffered, however, it was no longer possible to believe in him implicitly by believing in the Savior whom God would send, since Christ was no longer the Savior whom God would send, but rather the Savior whom God had already sent. But nor was it possible to believe in Christ implicitly after the passion by saying that one believed in the Savior whom God might or might not have already sent, for this is not in fact an act of faith in the Savior, since it abstracts from the question of his very existence. It is simply a readiness to believe, not an act of faith. And nor is it possible to believe in Christ implicitly by saying, I believe in the Savior who has already come, but I know nothing at all about him, as this assertion contains a contradiction. For when one holds that the Savior has already come and saved mankind, one does so ultimately either by one's own experience of him, or through the testimony of those who themselves saw and knew him. And this testimony is to a certain man who lived on earth at a certain time and place and performed and suffered certain things. Therefore, the faith becomes by means of such testimony, and much more the faith that comes by direct sense experience of him, would no longer be implicit faith, but rather explicit faith.

I conclude then, that there is, since the death of Christ on the Cross, no such thing as implicit faith in him. But since faith in him is at all times necessary for salvation, and since implicit faith in him is no longer possible, I conclude that explicit faith in Christ is necessary to please God, and therefore not simply believing that God exists and rewards those who seek him.

REPLIES TO THE ARGUMENTS OF THE PROPOSITION

I come now to the arguments that were put forward on both sides.

AD PROP. 1. The first argument was that the existence of God contains all divine perfections and his providence comprises all his effects towards creatures, and therefore whoever believes in his existence and his providence is always (to use the term of the arguer) "virtually" believing in all that can be believed, and therefore must be believing in all that has to be believed. I answer that, because our faith has, in order to make us pleasing to God, to bring us to God, and that because we are by nature in a state of sin, we need to believe in God not simply as one who can deliver us if he so chooses, but in one who actually wills to deliver us from sin, for only by so doing do we come to him in a way that pleases him. So, somewhat similarly, to be healed by a doctor, it is not enough to believe that the doctor can cure us if he so chooses, but we must *actually go* to him. And in the case of God, we go to him by faith in his will to save us, not simply in his absolute power to do so.

AD PROP. 2. The second argument was that Adam and Eve would have been pleasing to God if they had not

sinned, and their descendants would have been pleasing
to God likewise, though they would have simply been
believing that God exists and is a rewarder of those who
seek him. I answer that, even if this is so, it does not
directly relate to our question, since we are asking about
what actually is and not what could have been.

AD PROP. 3. The third argument is that the Apostle
in Hebrews II gives us several heroes of faith in the Old
Testament, such as Joshua and Noah, of whom it is not
narrated that they believed in more than God's existence
and providence. And therefore God would be giving us
insufficient examples if it was necessary to believe in more
than these two things. I answer that it is narrated of these
people in the same place that they all died in hope, and
that hope, in the Scriptures, when mentioned absolutely,
refers to the hope of future supernatural beatitude, which
already goes beyond a mere belief in God's providence;
but that also these people showed by their sacrifices that
they were aware of the need for a deliverer, and that they
expressed their faith in a Redeemer by these sacrifices.

AD PROP. 4. The fourth argument was that Job pleased
God even though he was a Gentile and so only had natural reason; therefore, anyone who not only deduces
by natural reason that God exists and is a rewarder, but
instead of this believes on faith, must please God even
more because faith is more pleasing to God than natural
reason. I deny the premise because Job, though a Gentile, was not a pagan. That is to say, he had faith in the
true God, and as we see in his book, he believed in the
Redeemer and in the future resurrection.

AD PROP. 5. The fifth argument was that St. Paul blames
the Gentiles not for their ignorance of other truths than
that of God's existence. I answer that the intention of
the Apostle in that place, in Romans I, was to show the
depravity of man without the grace of God, and therefore he listed the worst sins. So we can conclude from
this passage that it is worse to be an atheist than to be

a theist who has no faith in Christ, but not that such a theist can be pleasing to God.

AD PROP. 6. The sixth argument was that *Lumen Gentium* 16 states that the plan of salvation also includes those who acknowledge the Creator. I answer that this quotation itself need mean nothing more than that such people receive the actual graces that will enable them to come to truths other than the truths of God's creation and providence.

REPLIES TO THE ARGUMENTS OF THE OPPOSITION

So now I come to the arguments in favor of the view that something more than belief in God and his being a rewarder is needed.

AD OPP. 1. The first one was that the Council of Florence, in its Decree for the Copts, states that pagans, Jews, and heretics need to be changed from their state before they can enter eternal life. They need to cease to be pagans, Jews, and heretics before the end of their life; and therefore some of these people do have belief in God and his being a rewarder; and therefore something more than these two beliefs must be necessary. To complete this argument one would have to add that the categories listed by Florence completely exhaust the categories of those who believe in these two propositions and do not believe in anything more than them. So I accept this argument while noting that it is not by supernatural faith that these categories of persons believe in the things that they do believe, apart from schismatics, whom I did not mention, but who are also mentioned by Florence. They can have supernatural faith but not charity if they are schismatics in the proper sense of the word.

AD OPP. 2. The second argument was also from Florence — that Florence defined the Athanasian Creed, and that this Creed teaches that belief in the Incarnation and the Trinity is necessary for salvation. I accept this argument, though I suggest that some further work may need to be done to demonstrate that the Athanasian Creed is speaking about a necessity of means and not of precept.

AD OPP. 3. The third argument quoted both from St. Peter, "that no other name is given under heaven by which we may be saved," and from the Catechism of the Catholic Church, "that believing in God and the one whom he sent for our salvation is necessary to obtain that salvation." I accept these arguments, though I would suggest that the passage from the Catechism of the Catholic Church could also be used by someone maintaining implicit faith in Christ as salvific even now. So some more work might need to be done by someone who wished to use that passage from the Catechism to deny implicit faith.

AD OPP. 4. The fourth argument was from Clement XI, who said that one should not baptize an adult pagan, even though he says he is willing to believe anything a missionary tells him, if he does not already know about the Trinity and the Incarnation because these are doctrines that are necessary by a necessity of means for obtaining salvation. So I accept this argument, since unless there were an absolute necessity of means there would seem to be no reason why baptism could not be given.

AD OPP. 5. The fifth argument was that the existence and providence of God can be known by reason; therefore it would follow from the thesis that grace and revelation are not needed; and therefore those maintaining the thesis would be upholding not the Gospel of grace, but the pride of Satan. I answer that this is a powerful argument, but that there might be need to rebut those who would say that the benefit of revelation comes from the fact that, in practice, no human being does naturally know all truths about God without admixture of error unless he is given a revelation.

AD OPP. 6. And I answer similarly for the sixth argument — that the Gospel would not be Good News, since it would neither be good nor news if the thesis were true; since it would not be *good*, as it would simply be imposing a new burden on us — the burden of believing in things that are not actually necessary for our salvation; and it would not be *news*, since we could know the content without revelation. So this, while I accept it as a powerful argument, would also need to meet the objection that was made in the rebuttals, that in practice, it is good and is news because, given that we are all a bit stupid without revelation, nobody actually knows everything he could theoretically know.

REPLIES TO THE REBUTTALS

So now, finally, I come to any remaining arguments from the rebuttals that have not been covered.

AD REB. 1. One was the argument that if the thesis were true, philosophers could not be saved, because they already know these two articles by natural reason and not by faith; and that this seems a bit hard on philosophers. I argue that this does not seem to follow, since they might have faith in some other articles.

AD REB. 2. It was also suggested that the argument from Romans 1 was that the Gentiles are being condemned for not knowing the existence of God. The defenders of the thesis were maintaining that, if God had wanted the Gentiles to believe in things beyond the naturally knowable truths, that St. Paul would have rebuked them for it. And someone opposing the thesis replied that the Gentiles, if they had believed in the existence of God and his providence, would not thereby have been pleasing to God, but would simply have been not foolish. But I argue that this is not really in accordance with the mind of St. Paul, and that he would think of Gentiles living after the passion of Christ as being foolish if they only believed in the providence of God and his existence and not in the salvation by Christ, because he says that God has made foolish the wisdom of the world, and the wisdom of the world is precisely the wisdom of the Gentile philosophers who believe in God but not in Christ.

AD REB. 3. Then an argument was put forward that the Jews and heretics denied God's governance because they deny the Church by which he rewards people, and therefore the fact that they are being said by Florence to be not partakers of eternal life unless they change their state before the end of their life, does not mean that one needs to believe in things other than God's existence and governance in order to be pleasing to God, because they do not even believe in God's existence and governance. But I say this does not follow, because from the fact that they deny the Church, in which as a matter of fact he rewards us, it does not follow that they deny God's will to reward.

AD REB. 4. Then it was said we should baptize anybody in danger of death and that the Church exhorts us to do this. But in fact this is only true of those below the age of reason. We should baptize any child who is unbaptized if he is about to die even if the parents try to stop us. But in the case of adults, they must be disposed in order to receive baptism, not only lawfully but even validly. And the Holy Office has said that such dispositions include belief in the Trinity and Incarnation.

AD REB. 5. Then it was said that if the thesis were not true, it would follow that God was not pleased by just and true and beliefs, such as beliefs in him and his providence. I answer that we have to distinguish senses of God's being pleased. In one sense he is pleased in all that is, and therefore all the more is he pleased in any spiritual truth. God is pleased even in an ant, and he is pleased in a judgment that two and two are four, but he is not pleased in the sense of bringing us into friendship with himself simply by the fact of a person believing in some true statement, even about God himself.

AD REB. 6. Then it was remarked that the Catechism of the Catholic Church states that the axiom that there is no salvation outside the Church is not referring to those who are in invincible ignorance of the need to belong to the Church. And I agree that those who are invincibly ignorant of the command to be members of the Church are not sinning by not belonging to the Church, but we're not talking in this question precisely about membership in the Church, but about explicit faith in Christ. And that can be had even by those who are invincibly ignorant of the command to enter the Catholic Church.

AD REB. 7. Then it was said that in *Lumen Gentium* (and quoted in the Catechism) there is reference to those who are ignorant of the Gospel and who can be led by ways known to God himself to salvation. And I answer that this is true, but we must not forget that the Gospel includes not only the divinity of Christ and the Incarnation but all the things that go along with it, such as the Church and the sacraments and all the other doctrines of the faith. So the fact that people could be ignorant of certain revealed truths and be saved does not prove that they could be ignorant of all revealed truths and be saved. And again, the Council is not precise in explaining what it means about God leading people by ways known to himself, people who are without the preaching of the Gospel, since it could be a reference to God enlightening someone without a human preacher, for example on their death bed, shortly before the departure of the soul, about the truths of Christ and the Trinity. So I say that we cannot conclude from Vatican II nor from the Catechism that the thesis is true.

Finis.

APPENDIX

St. Thomas's *Divisio Textus* of the Letter to the Hebrews

THE STRUCTURE OF THE EPISTLE TO THE HEBREWS ACCORDING TO ST. THOMAS AQUINAS

One letter, that to the Hebrews, considers the grace of Christ as it exists in the head of the body, Christ himself.

CAP. LECT.

1   1 I. 1:1–10:39 He extols Christ's grandeur to show the superiority of the New Testament over the Old

A. 1:1–6:20 He proves Christ's preeminence over the personnel of the Old Testament

1. 1:1–2:18 He proves Christ's preeminence over the angels

a. 1:1–3 He shows the excellence of Christ

i. 1:1–2a He shows Christ's excellence in virtue of his unique origin, by calling Him the true natural Son of God

ii. 1:2b He shows Christ's excellence in virtue of the extent of His rule

iii. 1:2c He shows Christ's excellence in virtue of the power of His activity

iv. 1:3 He shows Christ's excellence in virtue of the sublimity of His glory and dignity

A) He shows that Christ is worthy of His dignity

2   1) 1:3a He shows that Christ is worthy because of the ease with which He acts

2) 1:3b He shows that Christ is worthy because of His diligence and strenuousness in acting

B) 1:3c He discloses this dignity

b. 1:4–14 He shows how Christ's excellence exceeds the angels

3   i. 1:4–5 In His sonship

ii. 1:6–9 In His dominion

CAP. LECT.

4

A) 1:6 He describes His dominion
B) 1:7 He describes the nature of that dominion on the part of the angels
C) 1:8–9 He describes the nature of that dominion on the part of Christ
   1) 1:8–9a He commends Christ's royal dignity
   2) 1:9b He shows His fitness for it

5   **iii.** 1:10–12 In His power
6   **iv.** 1:13–14 In His honor

2 1 **iii.** 2:1–18 He concludes that Christ's doctrine, namely, the New Testament, deserves more obedience than the Old Testament
      i. 2:1 He states the conclusion intended
 2   **ii.** 2:2–4 He supports his conclusion with a reason
      iii. 2:5–18 He confirms the consequence
        A) 2:5 By showing that Christ's power is greater than that of the angels
        B) 2:6–18 He proves this on the authority of Scripture
           1) 2:6a He commends the value of the testimony to be adduced
           2) 2:6b–8a He adduces it
              a) 2:6 The mystery of His Incarnation
              b) 2:7a The mystery of His Passion
              c) 2:7b–8a The mystery of His Exaltation
           3) 2:8b–18 He explains the meaning of the testimony
              a) 2:8b He explains its sublimity
              b) 2:9–18 He explains its diminution, namely, that to be made "a little less than the angels" seems to

3   militate against his chief intention
                  i) 2:9 He shows in what sense the lessening is to be understood
                  ii) 2:10 He describes the suitability of the Passion
                  iii) 2:11–18 He proves what he has said

4   **(A)** 2:11–13 He proves his conclusion on the part of the Father sanctifying
                    (B) 2:14–18 He proves his conclusion on the part of the Son sanctified
                        (1) 2:14a He shows the condition of the nature through which He could suffer and die
                        (2) 2:14b–15 He shows the benefits He obtained by dying
                        (3) 2:16–18 He proves what he had proposed

CAP.	LECT.	
5	1	**3.** 5:1–6:20 He proves Christ's preeminence over the priesthood of the Old Testament
		a. 5:1–10 He shows that Christ is a high priest
		i. 5:1–4 He shows what is required of a high priest
		ii. 5:5–9 He shows that the aforesaid belongs to Christ
		A) 5:5–6 He shows that Christ was made a high priest not by Himself but by God
	2	**B)** 5:7 He treats of his office
		C) 5:8–9 He treats of his mercy
		iii. 5:10 He concludes that Christ is a high priest
		b. 5:11–6:20 He prepares his hearers for what follows
		i. 5:11–14 He shows their slowness
		A) 5:11a He shows the importance of what is to be said
		B) 5:11b–14 He shows their slowness
6	1	**ii.** 6:1–20 He returns to his theme by stating his intention
		A) 6:1–2 He discloses his intention: to pass over those things which pertain to the beginning of Christian doctrine in order to treat of loftier matters
		B) 6:3–8 He shows its difficulty — both in itself and in relation to his hearers
		1) 6:3 He suggests that in this he especially needs divine help
		2) 6:4–6 He mentions their weakness
		a) 6:4–5 He lists the good things they had received
		b) 6:6a He states the difficulty caused in them from recurring
		c) 6:6b He assigns the reason (their guilt)
	2	**3)** 6:7–8 He proposes a simile
	3	**C)** 6:9–20 He declares his intention, namely, to snatch them from danger
		1) 6:9 He shows the confidence he had in them
		2) 6:10–20 He shows the reasons for this confidence
		a) 6:10–12 One, on their past good works
	4	**b)** 6:13–20 The other, on God's promise
7	1	**iii.** 7:1–10:39 He returns to his main theme: to prove the excellence of Christ's priesthood over the Levitical priesthood
		i. 7:1–28 He shows the prerogative of Christ's priesthood over the Levitical on the part of the person
		A) 7:1–25 He proves the existence of Christ's priesthood by reason of a divine promise
		1) 7:1–3 He shows the likeness of Christ to Melchizedek

CAP. LECT.

11　1　II. 11:1–13:25 He discusses what unites the members to the head, namely, faith
　　　　　A. 11:1 He describes faith
　　2　　B. 11:2–40 He gives various examples of it
　　　　　　1. 11:2 He manifests his thesis in general
　　　　　　2. 11:3–40 He manifests his thesis in detail with examples of the ancients
　　　　　　　a. 11:3 As to what they believed and taught
　　　　　　　b. 11:4–35a As to what they did
　　3　　　　　i. 11:4–7 He shows what the fathers did who lived before the deluge
　　　　　　　　ii. 11:8–23 He shows what the fathers did who lived before the Law
　　　　　　　　　A) 11:8–19 He shows what Abraham did
　　　　　　　　　　1) 11:8–16 He shows what Abraham did with regard to external and human knowledge
　　　　　　　　　　　a) 11:8–10 He shows what Abraham did in regard to his dwelling place
　　　　　　　　　　　b) 11:11–12 He shows what Abraham did in regard to generation
　　4　　　　　　　　c) 11:13–16 He shows what Abraham did in regard to his own conversion
　　　　　　　　　　2) 11:17–19 He shows what Abraham did with regard to God
　　5　　　　　　B) 11:20 He shows what Isaac did
　　　　　　　　　C) 11:21–23 He shows what Jacob and his sons did
　　　　　　　　iii. 11:24–35a He shows what the fathers did who lived under the Law, divided into three parts
　　6　　　　　　A) 11:24–26 Before the departure from Egypt
　　7　　　　　　B) 11:27–31 During the departure
　　　　　　　　　C) 11:32–35a What happened in the promised land
　　　　　　　　　　1) 11:32 He gives the names of the fathers and the reason why he passes over their deeds quickly
　　　　　　　　　　2) 11:33a He shows what they did by faith
　　8　　　　　　　3) 11:33b–35a He shows what they received by faith
　　　　　　　c. 11:35b–40 As to what they suffered
　　　　　　　　i. 11:35b–38 He shows how they suffered for the faith
　　　　　　　　ii. 11:39–40 He shows how the promises made to them were deferred
12　1　　C. 12:1–13:25 He gives a moral exhortation to keep the faith in their hearts and show it in their works
　　　　　　1. 12:1–29 He teaches how they should behave in regard to evil

CAP.	LECT.	
	2	**a.** 12:1–11 He teaches how they should behave in regard to tolerating evils of chastisement
		i. 12:1 He gives the example of the ancients
		ii. 12:2–4 He gives the example of Christ
		iii. 12:5–11 He quotes the authority of Scripture
	3	**A)** 12:5–6 He gives the authority
		B) 12:7 He explains its meaning
		C) 12:8–11 He argues to his conclusion
		b. 12:12–29 He teaches how they should behave in regard to avoiding the evils of guilt
		i. 12:12–17 He gives his admonition
		A) 12:12–13 He warns men who sin
	4	**B)** 12:14–17 He warns those not yet sinning
		ii. 12:18–29 He gives the reasons for his admonition
		A) 12:18–24 He makes a comparison between the Old and New Testaments
	5	**B)** 12:25–29 He argues from the comparison and draws a conclusion
13	1	**2.** 13:1–25 He teaches how they should behave in regard to good
		a. 13:1–19 He urges them to good
		i. 13:1–3 He shows them how to do good to their neighbor
		ii. 13:4–6 He shows them how to do good to themselves
		iii. 13:7–19 He shows them how to do good to prelates
		A) 13:7–16 He shows how they should act in regard to their dead prelates, namely, follow their example
	2	**1)** 13:7–8 He shows how they should follow the teachings of the good
	3	**2)** 13:9–16 He shows how to avoid the doctrine of evil
		B) 13:17–19 He shows them how they should act in regard to their living prelates, namely, obey them
		1) 13:17 How to act in regards others
		2) 13:18–19 How to act in regard to Paul himself
		b. 13:20–25 He prays for them

www.ingramcontent.com/pod-product-compliance
Lightning Source LLC
Chambersburg PA
CBHW030251130626
46549CB00002B/490

* 9 7 8 1 9 6 5 3 0 3 8 8 7 *